CW00765474

A Conscious Humanity

Morality, Freedom & Natural Law

Rob Ryder & Patrick Quanten

Disclaimer

CONTENTS

Paul

Thanks for our interesting conversations

all the best

Rob

"*Believe nothing. No matter where you read it or who said it, not even if I have said it, unless it agrees with your own reason and your own common sense.*"

Buddha

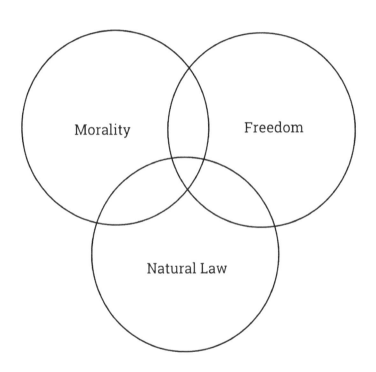

INTRODUCTION

The writing of this book is taking place in the middle of the biggest psychological attack on mankind ever. The truth is, mankind has always been under this attack, only now, with modern technology, it is happening on a global scale – and just about nobody is left unscathed… that is, if it hasn't killed them (yes, people are dispensable under this control system).

For as long as we know there has never been true freedom on this planet for the individual. It doesn't really matter how far back you go, or where geographically we look, all we see is the tentacles of control in many different forms. We have seen the "divine right to rule" expressing itself through Pharaohs, Emperors, Kings and Queens and other Monarchs, with a religious priesthood working alongside these or even leading the way.

This form of rule can be seen easily throughout European, Middle-Eastern and Asian history, but control can also be seen throughout Central and South America, and in fact, globally. People don't tend to think of indigenous peoples having this form of control over its people. But whatever group of people you look at, there will always be a system of control and a hierarchy or superstitious belief, though not all about domination.

In modern times, we have institutions called "Governments" which manifest in many forms, from communism to fascism, and dictatorships to democracies – with democracies supposedly equating to freedom (more on this later).

The truth is, history has always been written by the victors. Thus what we are told about the history of mankind on this planet is at best an opinion, and at worst, and outright lie.

Neither of us profess to know the true history of mankind. But there are many researchers who have done extensive studies over many decades who we contend have put forward more truthful versions of history.

We aren't looking to do that. Our intention is to give you ONE TRUTH that nobody can dispute:

Your life is your own.

This one simple truth may seem obvious. Yet in practice, most of humanity seem to accept and even condone slavery – almost as if they don't believe that your life *is* your own.

In his book *Medical Fascism: How coronavirus policies took away our freedoms and how to get them back* Rob Ryder puts forward compelling scientific data about disease and vaccines, and the truth about allopathic thinking and its drugs and treatments and how this is fuelling the insanity taking place across the planet right now.

The book goes into detail about medical science but only a small amount regarding mind control and the psychological attack. This book sets out to further explore this aspect of the many insidious attempts to undermine the truth: that your life is your own. In the book *Why me? Science and Spirituality as*

Inevitable Bed Partners Dr Patrick Quanten and Erik Bualda show in great detail creation, how it happens, its purpose and the role of the human being in this divine manifestation of potential.

The individual spirituality meets the world of science as we, the people, get to know more about the reality of life itself. Only through such knowledge and awareness can the individual, and through the individual humanity itself, evolve towards its full potential.

A Conscious Humanity is meant "to cut through the crap" and just give simple truths.

There are many researchers who may have published more detailed work on mind control and the human condition. We recommend you do that research, but sometimes too much information clouds the message and in truth there is only one thing at stake on this planet for humanity:

Freedom of the Individual.

A Conscious Humanity simplifies what the other research points to, so that you have accessible and usable information you can use in your fight to reclaim your individual freedom.

When you make up a jigsaw puzzle you are aware it is made up of many pieces and that those pieces make up one big picture. When focusing on the smaller pieces many people lose sight of the big picture.

This book brings these pieces together so you can see the big picture.

The big picture shows humanity in slavery and the truth is it is a slavery we have built ourselves and maintain ourselves. Now is the time to break free, and while most people are looking outside of themselves, observing problems and looking for solutions, we aim to encourage people to look closer to home – to discover the root of our problems and consequently to find the solutions. Yes, we will touch on the fact there are elites manipulating humanity in various ways, but we will keep the focus on us as individuals, as that is where the real understanding and solutions lie.

> *"If we can really understand the problem, the answer will come out of it, because the answer is not separate from the problem."*
>
> ### Jiddu Krishnamurti

The real truth about the nature of humanity and its problems, and our own, needs to be understood before we can even think about solving these said problems. The external wars in reality are a manifestation of the wars going on in our own minds. The real war is the war on the consciousness of the individual human being. A harsh truth needs to be accepted before we can even contemplate solving the riddle. By solving the riddle the truth will be revealed, and by revealing the truth the truth will be changed.

We are all slaves.

To free ourselves from slavery we need to know what is enslaving us. To know this, we need to know who we are and why we behave, and are manipulated to behave, in the way we do. Only then it is possible to end the insanity and to live in a world where real freedom exists and where humanity can really find out what living is all about.

Join us on our journey.

TERMINOLOGY

Morality

Morality is a set of principles guiding us to evaluate that what is right or wrong, and it builds the personal character, reasonable behaviour and choices of a person as well as helping people to justify decisions, goals, and actions all through life.

Normatively to refer to a code of conduct that, given specified conditions, would be put forward by all rational people.

Morality can be a body of standards or principles derived from a code of conduct from a particular philosophy, religion or culture, or it can derive from a standard that a person believes should be universal. Morality may also be specifically synonymous with "goodness" or "rightness".

Immorality

Behaviour that conscientiously goes against accepted morals, that is, the proper ideas and beliefs about how to behave in a way that is considered right and good by the majority of people.

Immorality is often called wickedness and is a state avoided by good people.

The quality of not being in accord with standards of right or good conduct.

Freedom

The state of being free or at liberty rather than in confinement or under physical restraint.

Exemption from external control.

The power to determine action without restraint of any kind.

Slavery

Modern slavery refers to situations of exploitation in which a person cannot refuse or leave because of threats, violence, coercion, deception, or abuse of power.

Slaves are obliged to live their lives in perpetual service to their master, an obligation that only the master (or the state) can dissolve.

Slavery, a condition in which one human being was owned by another. A slave was considered by law as property, or chattel, and was deprived of most of the rights ordinarily held by free persons.

Natural Law

Based upon principles and truth. (Inherent to creation).

Harmonized with, due to knowledge and understanding.

Universal; exists and applies anywhere in the Universe regardless of location.

Eternal and immutable; exists and applies for as long as the Universe exists, and cannot be changed.

Man-made Law

Based upon dogmatic beliefs. (Constructs of the mind).
Complied with, due to fear of punishment.
Differs with location based upon the whim of legislators. (Moral Relativism)
Changes with time based upon the whim of legislators. (Moral Relativism).

Note – The Natural Law definition is from researcher Mark Passio who has been researching Natural Law for over 14 years. His work can be found at www.whatonearthishappening.com

THE SEARCH FOR TRUTH

Patrick Quanten

I wanted to become a doctor because I was convinced that if one knows the answers to all diseases and if one could cure all those diseases, the world should be free of them. I thought that if, as a doctor, I would do my job well, people would no longer be suffering from illnesses. My ideal was to do my job that well so that I, and my colleagues, would be out of a job. It didn't work out that way!

I discovered that no treatment that I learned about worked for everybody all the time. And this was no different when I started investigating the alternative treatments. So I kept looking for answers, as I began to realise that I must be missing an important point somewhere. I began to study life itself. So I evolved from occupying myself with diseases, to becoming more and more interested in health, to wanting to understand life much better.

Studying life showed me a lot of things that are wrong with the way humans are told to live. I no longer believed any sources I drew information from. Instead I started to combine similar information about life itself to try and puzzle things together in a way I could comprehend and that I could justify and keep justifying to myself.

In order to have the freedom to investigate life the way I wanted to, in order to become free from oppressing ideas and dogmas, I turned my back on the profession I worked so hard to be part of. I turned away from every organisation I ever came across and I vowed never to be part of any group anymore, never to feel the restrictions of the beliefs others may hold. Now I was free. Now I was alone.

I soon found out that this also means that nobody listens to you anymore. Yet, I continued because I enjoyed the freedom to think independently. I embraced the fact that if I was going to be wrong, at least it would all have been my own mistake and not because someone else convinced me of something.

This is where I am, and this is where you are. For you to know whether someone is telling the truth or not, or to put it differently, whether someone else's conviction contains real truth, you need to investigate and collate your own evidence. For you to make up your own mind as to what you would like to believe, you have a free choice. You are free to base it on any information you care to consider.

When someone is telling you something totally different from what you believe, you have a choice. Either this person is completely nuts, or this person has learned something you don't yet know.

When two opinions are being expressed that are totally opposed, there are only three possibilities. And only one of them is true, irrespective of what you believe. One, this person is right and the other one is wrong. Two, the other person is right and this person is wrong. And three, they are both wrong.

Your choice. You believe whatever suits you best. Whatever you believe does not alter the truth. In order to find the truth, you will have to search it out – and often will find it in unexpected places, away from mainstream narratives, sometimes even hidden from view. The bottom line is: if you seek truth, you'll have to do the digging.

Seek and you will find.
Ask and you will be given.

SOMETHING DIDN'T FEEL RIGHT...

Rob Ryder

I was born in 1969 in a council estate in Manchester called Wythenshawe. For many people it would seem we were poor. In those days there was no central heating, no double glazing and, at least for us, no carpets. We lived on the third floor – the top floor – of a small block of flats. My "mam" (mother) was a single parent to me and my elder brother (many of my neighbourhood friends were in the same situation). We typically lived off beans on toast, spaghetti on toast, egg and chips, and homemade mushy peas – and sometimes an orange at night when we'd settled down after a bath to watch the black and white television set. In those days TVs only had three channels available and had to warm up before the picture appeared. If it didn't work for some reason, you'd give it a whack with your hand on the top or the side. To this day no technical expert has been able to tell me how whacking a TV made it work – but it did.

Sometimes when the electricity meter needed topping up, but we didn't have the money to do so, my mam made a 50 pence coin shape from a piece of vinyl record, which fitted the slot and would get us through the night. We had many nights without electric before we found out that trick. I'm sure those records would have been worth a few quid by now if they hadn't been cut up! The only thing my mam had to do was make sure the amount of plastic money in the meter was available in real money by the time the meter man came around to empty it.

My daily routine was just going out to play. I didn't have to go far as my friend Leigh lived just across the hall in the opposite top flat. We would play all day up and down the stairs and never found ourselves bored or unable to find something to do.

When we were a little older, my brother, Leigh, and I would play with the kids from some nearby flats. Most days we'd go to the park across the road. It was a good-sized park with a playground and plenty of trees to climb and have adventures on. We'd go home when we were hungry or when it was getting dark. Getting older, we'd mostly play football with the odd game of cricket during summer months.

It was a lively place to live and grow up in – and it was all I knew. None of us even thought about life anywhere else in Britain, never mind other parts of the world. The estate was my only reality. I remember someone taking his life by jumping of the roof from the big block of flats, about ten stories high. I also remember excitedly following the blood trail after someone had been axed in the head outside our flats. To this day, I'm not sure whether he survived or not. The blood trial went in the direction of Wythenshawe Hospital which was just half a mile away. There was never a dull moment.

Some people complain about how they were poor when they were growing up and how bad their environment was.

Some people may read this and think the same. Rubbish. A child has no understanding of being poor, at least in a material sense, unless they have something to *compare* their life to. I certainly had no conception of us being poor. Even getting second hand clothes from a jumble sale gave me no impression we had little money. A child doesn't need much in the material sense. A child who feels safe and secure in his or her home and has the freedom to play is the richest child in the world. It is only when we get older, and we compare ourselves to others and hanker after material things, that we recognize that we grew up close to the breadline. It's become trendy nowadays for stars and celebrities to highlight how they grew up in poor backgrounds – before they "made it" (made what exactly? I'm not sure). I doubt their younger selves had any notion that they were living in poverty.

We may never have had the material goods and home comforts people have now, but we were certainly rich in life. We may have lived in a cold flat with damp walls (which was bad for my asthma – and absolutely bitter in Manchester winters) but it was warmed up by the security of knowing mam was always there. Having known people who have suffered terrible abusive childhoods, I can tell you all the material things in the world are nothing if a child is not safe and loved. Real poverty is a lack of love and security. My life was pretty normal (whatever that means), until the last year of school when something changed…

I had always enjoyed school, mostly seeing it as a place to go and play with my friends. In between playing football in the playground, we'd go inside to do some "work". To be fair, I quite enjoyed studying and could even say maths was my favourite subject after P.E (physical education). But during my last year of school things felt different. At the time I couldn't have said what seemed different. It was just something didn't *feel* right. During that last year I embraced the subjects I enjoyed and simply didn't work or even turn up for the lessons I didn't like.

I remember we gave our metalwork teacher a terrible time during the last year. The whole class simply would not work, and the teacher, after trying to scare us, just gave up. He managed to get us to do some work when we wanted to make net pegs for the football netting we used at home on weekends. We'd stolen the netting from a pitch after the Sunday league team had gone for a shower at full time. Not a good thing to do I know, but kids will be kids, and we were lucky we didn't get caught.

Then I remember something called PSE (Personal and Social Education). It came in during our last year. I remember going to one lesson and thinking it was utter nonsense. For the rest of the year when it was PSE, a handful of friends and I would jump the fence and wander around out of school until the time the lesson was over. We'd then head back for the final parts of the PSE lesson. PSE was always after lunch, so we just signed the register so it looked like we'd attended the lessons. You could do that in those days. I did attend the odd PSE class. It seemed lame and went over my head, and seemed to be about civic responsibility and social behaviour. It wasn't for us, thus we jumped the school fence and played in the woods instead.

Throughout the last year of school, I couldn't wait to leave. Why? I didn't know But I was done with it. I worked hard in the subjects I liked and got five O levels, which were pretty good grades. But I failed badly in the subjects I didn't enjoy, which was down to a complete lack of effort on my part. Essentially that last year was preparation for the "real world" and it was time to grow up. Thus a lot of lessons were geared to showing us how to apply for college or jobs. None of that was for me. I just wanted to leave school, go out and play football and get up when I felt like it. Basically to do what I liked, when I liked.

After leaving school my friends and I got jobs picking tomatoes for one pound an hour. Not a bad job and good money for kids who had never had any. Sadly, that didn't last long as we all got sacked for having a tomato fight. After that I got a job with my football team manager at his glazing firm. Again it paid one pound an hour and offered the chance of becoming a full time job. After a few months of this relative freedom, I received a letter from a bank I'd applied to for a job while still at school. They offered me a job, which held the promise of a secure career. Excited at the opportunity of making money, and having always enjoyed numbers and math, I took the job and embraced the rat race at seventeen. It was great at first. The salary enabled me to pass my driver's test, buy a car, and all the clothes I wanted – along with nights out and going on holidays.

I remember my first trip abroad with my friends – the "lads." After the plane landed in Tenerife, I vividly recall feeling the hot dry air on my face, seeing the blue skies and clear waters of the sea, and I just thought "this is for me". Manchester had been my whole life and I'd never imagined ever leaving the city. But his was something else.

Learning to drink alcohol was a key part of growing up in working class England. I'm sure my friends and I would have some good stories to tell if we could remember any of them. The general "wisdom" was if you could remember what happened, it couldn't have been a good night.

After two years or so working at the bar, I started to get the feeling that something was not right – just like happened in my last year at school. I remember sitting at a table at work talking to a really nice older guy who was coming up to retirement. He'd been at the bank all his life This had enable him to pay off his mortgage, run a good quality car, and take regular holidays. In short he'd got financial security and appeared to be proud and content with the life he'd created for himself. As we talked, I looked at him and thought, "this is not for me". It was as though I'd been show my whole future if I continued working at the bank. My life had been mapped out and I could see myself, forty years in the future, telling a new recruit exactly the same things as this guy was telling me.

The feeling of dissatisfaction had returned and I found myself simply going through the motions at work and yearning for the weekend to arrive so I could go out with my friends. About a year later I said to my colleagues at work that "I won't be here when I'm twenty-one". I can't remember if I planned it that way or if it just happened but I'm sure I left on my 21st birthday. No money saved up, no job to go to, no plans. I just walked out of a secure career with nothing except my last pay packet. I'd got my freedom again, except this time I was skint.

I soon got a job at Mr Kipling cakes, a well-known British brand. It was four hours a day at the minimum wage – but you could have all the cakes you wanted at cost price. It felt like I'd landed on my feet. The job didn't last too long, though. I struggled to keep up on the conveyor belt, and had difficulty sorting out the different flavours of jam tarts. You had to put one of each in tray, something that the women seemed to do without even looking, while holding a conversion at the same time.

As luck would have it, a friend of mine offered me a job window cleaning. Along with my friend Paul, I saved enough money to go and live in Greece as "beach bums". We'd had enough of working in dull jobs. We want sun, sand, and whatever else springs to mind that begins with "s".

I'd had a couple of holidays in Tenerife while working at the bank. So following the sun sounded good to me. There's something about the sun – the hot sun – that strongly appeals to me.

Our plan was to spend at least six months in the sun and maybe move on from there. Other than buying tickets to Corfu, we made no plans and did no research, which turned out to be a bad move. We got to Corfu early in the holiday season when most places were still closed. It was good weather; 22°C in the shade but you still a nice tan. On the first night, we went out for a meal and a beer and I pulled out my return ticket and set fire to it on the table. Paul, laughing, was now forced to do the same. We were in it together. As it turned out, our dreams and expectations only lasted a few weeks.

After going out drinking every night and then getting a job that paid in shots of ouzo and another that paid commission selling booze cruise tickets, we ended up penniless, with nowhere to live. We even sold our spare clothes and unimportant belongings to a family of Albanians who were in Greece working. Yes, we were poorer than the poorest people in Europe. The money from the two jobs did get us through another few days of pretty much living off bread and water.

We sometimes helped girls who were going home carrying their bags to the coach and they would give us their leftover food. I remember once eating Kellogg's Frosties cereal on dried bread, a sad sugar, but flavourless "treat". Things were bad. But we still had our job that paid ouzo so we could still have a night out. We even managed to sell a few booze cruise tickets, but we had to give all the money back as it got cancelled due to lack of sales. Even in Greece, especially early season, it can get cold at night. After many shots of ouzo and wearing only shorts and shirts, sleeping on the beach was not a nice experience. In fact, you couldn't sleep due to the cold. We spent most of the night praying for the sun to come up.

We then took to talking girls into giving us a warm bed for the night.

All we yearned for was to sleep under warm covers. We had nothing else in mind with the girls, – only for them to take pity on us and give us some respite from the cold. It was a great crazy time, but we were totally clueless and inept when it came to managing what money we had. After six weeks, most of them spent homeless, we'd had enough.

It came to a head when another English beach bum and I broke into a half-finished hotel for the night in order to sleep on the floor with cardboard for blankets.

Another friend had said goodbye to his latest girlfriend and knew her apartment would be empty. He sneaked in with a fellow homeless friend thinking they would at least have a bed each, even if only for one night. As it turned out, the new arrivals entered the apartment early the next morning and so the two both jumped out of the balcony on the first floor to the ground to escape. One of the guys fell badly and broke his ankle. We met up in the main street as usual the next day and found him there in pain with a cast on his ankle. Things were starting to get serious and the fun was wearing off.

Paul and I had kept £100 each that we agreed would only be for emergencies. The emergency, we decided, was to get home. With the season still not yet in full swing and no immediate chance of making money we decided hunger, cold and breaking ankles wasn't much fun anymore. Without tickets we managed to get home with a ticket trick that was used a lot by the workers who went there every year. With modern technology it would not be possible anymore. I'll say no more.

Not long after getting back, Paul moved over to Jersey in the Channel Islands and I was back cleaning windows. Feeling bored again, I had a chat will Paul and he arranged a job for me at the hotel his football manager ran. In Jersey they were fanatical about football and as I was a reasonable player, the hotel manager gave me a job knowing I'd be keen to also play in the football team. The job got me through the summer holiday season. After that, I secured a full-time job at the Blue Note Bar.

Feeling settled, I enjoyed this new lifestyle. I was on an island paradise, making good money, enjoying a great social life and great weather. After around two years working in Jersey, I got the "something doesn't feel right" sensation again. I just needed to get away. I still couldn't explain why. I had a great job, worked with great people, had plenty of money, and Jersey was undoubtedly a beautiful island. Yet I just didn't want to be there anymore.

Paul and I had a chat and decided we'd try traveling again. America was to be our destination this time. Once we'd saved enough money, we handed in our notices and bought tickets to Florida. We hadn't learnt learned our lessons from the debacle in Greece – and again did no research. We simply headed for Daytona Beach as it was famous and we presumed things would just work out for us.

We landed in Orlando and spent a week exploring the parks. Then we headed for Daytona. At first, things were fine. We found a cheap motel on the beach and one night we saw the space shuttle blasting off into the night sky right outside our door. After a week or so the manager told us that this was the last cheap week as "Spring Break was about to begin and thousands of college kids would arrive from all over the United States to party. This was music to our ears offering the chance for some fun and potentially work too. We managed to get a small room at the back of the motel at a reasonable price, but it wouldn't last long with the little money we had. Had we planned ahead we would have known this. But like last time we would have to pay the price for our lack of foresight

We were able to stay another couple of weeks at the motel, but Paul had decided he'd had enough. I'd got well over a grand left, so I was going to stay in Florida. As it was the two of us went back to Orlando for a week, which was cheaper. After that, went on his way. And now I was on my own.

I explored Orlando for a few days, visiting the few British pubs at night. I decided to call a girl I'd met in Greece. She was a teacher on holiday with her friends in Greece. She was one of the people I'd sold a booze cruise ticket to and had to refund to as the cruise didn't sail. She remembered me as that English bum sleeping on the beach and having fun without a care in the world.

I called her in Texas where she was now living. I told her I was in Orlando and looking for something adventurous to do and thought it would be nice for us to meet up after all this time and catch up. She agreed and invited me over to Texas. I looked at the map and it seemed a long way for one bus trip, so I told her I would stop off on the way in New Orleans as it was about half way.

The Blue Note Bar in Jersey was a live jazz bar and I had come to like the music and thought this would be a great place to see the home of the blues and have a night out along Bourbon Street. After making plans for Texas, I then boarded the Greyhound for New Orleans. I had a window seat which gave me great views of the changing countryside and criss-crossing highways. As I surveyed all this, a feeling came over me again. But this time it wasn't uncomfortable. It was a feeling of unknowing and excitement at the same time. I wouldn't have been able to explain it that way at the time, but I sensed something was different. It was a feeling of being free and "in the now". I was on a bus to New Orleans and that was all I knew. I had no conscious thought of the past or my future plan of visiting my friend in Texas. Both seemed to be totally irrelevant. I was on a bus traveling to New Orleans and that was it.

Arriving in New Orleans, I was somewhat nervous as I had heard of its very high crime rate. I'd been warned to be careful and not to wander down the wrong road, or even be on the wrong side of the road, as some of the people in the black ghettos would have a little white English guy for breakfast. I got off the bus and straight away forgot all the warnings and ended up walking about a mile to a backpackers I had heard about. I got there safely enough and checked into my dorm.

To my surprise the guy on the bunk next to me was from Jersey in the Channel Islands. We got chatting and it turned out he was working in the French Quarter. Never one to turn down the chance of a few beers, I arranged to meet him after his shift and take in the music and culture that was on offer. I wasn't disappointed. The music, architecture, culture, and atmosphere were just as I expected - even better than I expected. You could wander around the packed streets, warmed by the Southern heat. It was expensive to go into a bar to listen to music, but as they were all open you could take it all in from the street and the takeaway beer was cheap. I fell in love with New Orleans so much that I put Texas to the back of my mind. After about two weeks of "going out for a few beers" with new people from the backpackers it became clear to me my money was running out and I wouldn't make it to Texas. I phoned Sandy to tell her the news, which didn't surprise her at all as she knew me from my Greece days. I headed back to Florida for the last week, where I spent time in beautiful Clearwater Beach before heading back to Manchester, after a stay of two months.

The next few years went the same way as before, with me going to and from Manchester regularly. I was always able to pick up window cleaning jobs which kept me going while at home. Once I'd saved some money I'd head off again to a new place and new job. But again, after the newness of the surroundings, people, and job had worn off, I'd feel the urge to leave again. the urge to leave came around again. Only now this feeling came upon me quicker each time. I still wasn't sure what it was, but I could now understand it was what people call being trapped in the "rat race".

During the spring of 1998, I was back in Jersey and things weren't going well personally and I just said "fuck it". This is what my friend Chris and I back home in Manchester used to say when we were just about to do something stupid and knew there may be consequences, but knew we had to do it anyway. *"Fuck off, I'm off".*

I'd always fancied a big world trip but had never quite gotten around to it. It was now or never. So I gave myself the summer to save up the money. I secured a job as a waiter at Pizza Express in St. Helier. It was the busiest restaurant outside of London and I knew the tips were really good. I had plenty of experience now in catering and was just about the fastest, most efficient, waiter around. I had speed of foot and speed of thought. I'd figured out it was all about efficiency of movement and never wasting a trip. "Never go into the kitchen empty handed," I was told by an older guy who used to work on cruise ships. Add being cheeky in a polite and respectful way and I knew the money would roll in.

It all went as planned and by the middle of August I had the necessary money. I handed in my notice and said to my friends at the Blue Note Bar that I was off to New York and was planning to spend the New Year in Rio on the Copacabana Beach. They thought I was crazy but when I told them I meant New Year 2000 they thought I had lost the plot completely. I don't think they fully believed me until the morning of my flight to New York when I came in with my TV to give to a friend in the bar. I had one bag of clothes, my ticket and passport, and about £900. I didn't even give my notice in the room where I was living as I knew I wouldn't get my deposit back as I was supposed to give at least a month's notice. I left whatever clothes and belongings I could not take. I always wondered what the landlady thought had happened to me. Now you see him, now you don't.

So I was on my flight to New York with the plan of getting to Rio some 16 months away, and with only £900. Had I learnt my lessons of the past and done plenty of research to find my way on the challenging trip ahead? Nope.

Noel at the Blue Note told me to go to an Irish bar, called Kennedy's, in Manhattan and get some advice. But it turned out Manhattan sadly was out of my budget. A week later I was on a 36-hour bus journey to Miami in search of the sun.

To keep it short, with many adventures behind me throughout America, including another trip to New York, I finally met up with Sandy in Texas, spending a week there with her friend and boyfriend and enjoying the generous Texan hospitality. A few years late but I finally made it.

I spent the rest of the time exploring Mexico and Venezuela, before entering Brazil through the region of Roraima. I had now two fellow travellers with me, Dave from Australia, and Andy from Southport in the UK, whom I had met in Miami. We all agreed it was the Copacabana for the Millennium. After many incredible adventures we finally got to the beach two hours before midnight to fulfil our goal. For me it should have been the end of my dream trip but I still had a few thousand dollars left. Don't ask me how I had more money than when I started, but I began to realize it wasn't the end, but another new beginning.

I ended up in Lima, Peru, sometime in March 2000. Andy had already gone AWOL with a girl in Brazil and Dave and I were living it up with plans to keep moving. The end for me came fast. With one look at the girl in the main village I was gone, just like Mowgli, wandering behind the girl into the village. I didn't know it at the time, but my crazy irresponsible days were over.

I had seen the sunset at Key West, watched the divers plunge into the sea from the rocks in Acapulco, climbed the enormous Pyramids outside Mexico city, swam at the bottom of Angel Falls, climbed and walked the savannah at Mount Roraima, slept like sardines for days in hammocks on an Amazon river boat, kicked a football on the Copacabana, saw the amazing Iguazu Falls, crossed the Andes, taken the infamous illegal prison tour in La Paz before it was even infamous, went over 5000 metres crossing the Atacama Desert, visited the awe-inspiring Machu Pichu, flew over the mysterious Nasca Lines and had "a few beers" most nights along the way. Dave and I also got to see my hometown team Man United play in the famous Maracana stadium. I even had to explain to the Mexican immigration people I was actually in the country as they would not let me leave, because my passport had no stamp showing me entering the country. The fact I was standing right in front of them didn't seem to matter: "Passport says no!" After going to an office where I could get an entrance stamp, I was allowed to try again, this time proving beyond doubt I was in the country. I must have been in the country because this paper booklet now said I was.

This insanity at sticking to rules happened again at the border between Bolivia and Peru at the start of the crossing of the Atacama Desert over three nights in Land Rovers. A fellow traveller had the same problem, and couldn't convince the man in uniform at the tiny shack of an immigration office that he was actually there in front of him. Again: "Passport says no!" Being in the middle of nowhere, he wasn't as lucky as I was in Mexico City Airport, and he was sent back to La Paz to get confirmation he was in the country and therefore could leave with us.

This belief in rules and following orders has not only been responsible for hindering travellers, but also for making life difficult in many situations. Worse still, it has been partly responsible for countless genocides and atrocities committed against mankind throughout history and still to this day.

But my Achilles heel of the female Latin smile and dark eyes ended my carefree lifestyle. At least I'd a good run for my money. But marriage and even a daughter still couldn't get me to accept the routine of the normal life. When our daughter was five, we packed up and left England for Iquitos in Peru. A place I had never been to, but it was hot, cheap and apparently was a great laid-back town to settle down and live the easy life. I felt free again and things were fine - at least for me. A year later we returned to England to sort a few things out and get a bit more money, and Edith, my wife, decided she didn't want to go back. There were some things I could change to make life easier, but the heat and the mosquitos were things I could do nothing about. It was time to settle down at last, maybe.

These are just a few of the adventures I had before I "settled down". The point I am making is I had the opportunities to have a good amount of freedom in my younger days. A freedom all of us could and should have if we choose to. Yes, all of us. It wasn't my "white privilege" that allowed me to do what I did. We will come to that later.

You don't even have to travel to be free and experience life. We are all different and have different dreams and hopes for our lives. When Steve, Danny and I went to Zante for two weeks, Danny enjoyed it to the full, but after about ten days, he was ready to go back home. Steve embraced the full two weeks and I, as per usual, just wanted to stay in the sun. We are all different and all is good. We are all varied expressions of humanity and how we want and choose to live our lives is perfectly fine. Travelling and moving about isn't a better expression of freedom than just staying in your home town. It's just a different expression of that same freedom.

I chose to move about and was pushed by that feeling inside of being trapped. I still had many crazy times in Manchester and did all the stupid things young adults are supposed to do, and a few we are not meant to. These few silly stories are written down here to remind people that our children are being sold out into total slavery, a slavery where they will have no opportunity to travel, unless permitted to, and no opportunity to do all the silly things they need to do before they "grow up". Our children are being sold out so we can watch the football, go to the pub, have a holiday in the sun, or whatever other entertainment people put above freedom.

"Football, beer, and above all, gambling filled up the horizon of their minds. To keep them in control was not difficult…"

George Orwell, 1984

A TIME TO THINK

What settling down did after my Peruvian Amazon adventure was give me time to think and reflect on my experiences. It was funny that when I traced my journey in South America, it was almost the same as Che Guevara did on his famous motorcycle trip. I had started reading about his life and felt a close understanding of how he felt and why he did what he did. On reflection, it was very clear to me the immense corporate control that was over the governments and peoples of the continent. This control now I started to see worldwide.

I was then told to read a book called *The Open Veins of Latin America* by Eduardo Galeano, known as the bible of Latin American history. The way the corporate elite were taking over the world now became a bit clearer. Slavery was never abolished; it was rebranded as Free Trade. It is a big book with masses of historical information, but Galeano's words, "The Spanish had the cow, but it was others who drank the milk", sum up the whole conquest. It was always a corporate conquest, more to the point, a banking conquest.

Between the 16th and 18th century an unknown number of indigenous people from the Andes were worked to death by their corporate masters. Some estimates put the figure at eight million. This is a genocide or holocaust that the writers of mainstream history don't really want to remind us of. Why? Well maybe it highlights the unbelievable evil and cruelty of these elites, the same corporate elites who are still claiming ownership of land and people all over the world today, and who continue to cause environmental damage and human suffering on an immense scale. Those approximately eight million people worked to death were just a fraction of those who died over the whole continent. How these Elites gained this power will become much clearer as the book goes on, especially after the chapter on money creation.

I began to sympathise with the situation of the Cuban people under the US backed military dictatorship of Batista, and totally understood the actions of Castro and why he felt he had to act as he did. The situation they were in was fertile ground for a Marxist Revolution. If ever there was a clear case of oppressor and oppressed, this was it. It was a situation on one island that represented the suffering and exploitation of a whole continent, desperately waiting for some hero to save them from their misery. Castro was that man.

The revolution seemed to create a much fairer life for most Cubans. The main issue though, as I discovered, was that the Marxism that makes us identify our oppressor also brings us Marxism and socialism as a political solution. A solution that Communist Russia and China discovered kills tens of millions of people in the name of equality and justice. I decided to go to Cuba to see socialism in the flesh. It is fair to say there are many good things socialism has done in Cuba, such as education and healthcare, (I'll leave the issue with allopathic medicine aside), and a lack of homelessness, being some of the things the people appreciate. But when you have a quiet conversation with many Cubans after gaining their trust, it's clear the majority would like more economic freedom to pursue their own dreams and goals. This is something that is unbelievably controlled in Cuba. It may be a socialist paradise island on the surface but there is a tension bubbling underneath the surface, a tension I would understand more fully later on when I plunged into the world of the human experience.

In 2008 I decided to dive into the modern world and opened myself up to the internet and the mass of information on the World Wide Web. I could now ask the questions that I needed answers to. I could try and put this jigsaw puzzle of human suffering, and my own feeling of "something not quite right", together. Reading recommended books was great, but massively time consuming. With instant access to all the information needed, I began to investigate what my awareness allowed me. It soon became clear that the control of water, one of the basic human needs, was being taken over by the big corporations, and that the World Bank and the IMF (International Monetary Fund) would ask for water privatisation as part of the terms for loans.

Between 1997 and 2001 the privatisation of the Bolivian water supply and sanitation was a requirement of the World Bank if Bolivia were to continue to receive loans. At one point it even became illegal to collect rainwater. This cruel sell-out of the people by the political elite was their demise, and in 2005, leftist Evo Morales, the continent's first indigenous president, was elected. He was another one who had recognised the oppressors who were exploiting the people of his country and he decided to do something about it. This was a peaceful revolution. So this global corporate takeover of the world was becoming clearer. On the surface I completely understood the Marxist viewpoint of the suffering masses of Latin America, but as we know, an iceberg only reveals to us about 10% of its mass above the surface.

In 2008 the global financial crash exposed some of what had always been going on below the surface. Struggling to understand economics and the global financial markets, the 2008 crash exposed me to the real power behind the corporate machine and the elites who run it through money creation. I will focus a chapter on this later but it was the documentaries by American researcher Bill Still that opened my eyes to this scam of creating money out of thin air and issuing it as debt. His videos, "The Money Masters" and "The Secret of Oz" can still be found on YouTube with "Money as Debt" – another great documentary explaining this scam.

I then came across some real truths about 9-11 which tied in nicely with what I had found out about the bankers and the big corporations they supported and how terrorist attacks (allegedly committed by terrorists) could be used by world leaders to bring in laws to control their own people.

In 2009 I finally came across the information that explained my uneasy feeling about life. A talk by the late John Harris, still to be found on YouTube, entitled "It's an Illusion", gave me the simple truth about what enslaved me. My belief that I am my name. My belief that government and laws have real authority over me. And my belief that society is real. Again, this will be dealt with in full in a later chapter.

I was finally given the answer to the puzzle of why I had, since the age of fifteen, felt the way I did. It all became clear and a massive relief ensued. That relief was soon to be replaced with the obvious truth: I was a slave. A slave to a system that wasn't even real. But surely now I could see through the Illusion, it would be easy to break free. Just don't go along with the Illusion and it ceases to control me. Right? Wrong. The people who have devised this trick, this Illusion, were not going to let people walk away from it that easily. If I was single and had no responsibility, I could just put the middle finger up to the whole system and to hell with the consequences, but now I was a family man and people were depending on me. My life wasn't just about me doing as I pleased anymore.

That initial relief and momentary feeling of thinking I might reach that true freedom I searched for was over as quickly as it came. A new feeling of slavery came over me, a slavery I now understood, but could not escape. My family responsibility was far more important and meaningful, so like the character in George Orwell's *Keep the Aspidistra Flying*, I decided to embrace my slavery wholeheartedly.

The light of truth and freedom would not go out totally and I decided I was going to bring this lie into the public domain. Knowing John Harris had been talking about this stuff, I continued to research what he was doing and came across the UK Column alternative news channel in about 2010. I saw what they were doing on their website and that they had a newspaper being distributed throughout the UK. So it seemed a no brainer to help them distribute the paper rather than to start up something on my own with no experience and no resources. They were already up and running, had gained huge experience, knew what they were taking about, and were well organised. I contacted them and arranged to drive to Plymouth to have a chat and see what I could do. I remember Mike Robinson answering the phone. I was committed but asked him one question, the question we all face: "What are the consequences for my family by me going public about what I know?" The answer I already knew but I needed to hear it. "What are the consequences of doing nothing?" was the clear reply.

I knew the agenda of the monster that is controlling humanity. My research had gone deeper and it was clear something dark and sinister had plans for the human race. There was nowhere to hide. Keeping "under the radar", as some put it, was for me more dangerous than going public. I took a deep breath and decided it was all or nothing. I wasn't going to be reckless and knew I had to pick my battles wisely, but I decided it was safer to go public and speak the truth – making it clear I was taking a moral stance. I thought that would be my best protection. So now, with a good understanding of how the outside world functioned, I was actively doing something in an organised way and had made new friends locally who felt the same. It was very clear to me the banking system was the central point of control, but that behind the Bankers there was something very, very dark.

To really understand the human condition though, it is necessary to know what exactly a human being is. In 2011 I saw an interview with medical biochemist Trevor Gunn on alternative television. His simple explanation of illness not being the body going wrong, but simply responding intelligently to an issue, instantly made total sense. He also presented the screen data that showed the incidence numbers of what we call infectious diseases dropped dramatically, or totally, *before* vaccination began. The next day I ordered his book, *The Science of Health and Healing*, which took me on a journey to the inner world of the human body and mind. I then read Bruce Lipton's *The Biology of Belief* and Henry Lindlar's *Nature Cure*.

Also, since 2014, I started to work and arrange seminars in West Cornwall on matters relating to health and disease with former family Doctor Patrick Quanten. whom I found through my subscription to the Informed Parent. He was writing articles with the same understanding as in Trevor Gunn's book. This culminated in a seminar, which you'll find on Youtube by searching for: "Patrick Quanten – The creation and formation of a human being through opinions".

So I realised that to understand humanity I had to go to the foundation and ask the most basic question: what is a human being?

THE GAME OF LIFE

What is life?
Where does it come from?
How does it function?

This will be done as an illustration as it can be a simple way to get information across with meaning. The illustration of a gaming machine may not be 100% scientifically correct, but it's only meant to portray an idea.

- We have a player who has all the potential and imagination and wants to have an experience, but needs a vehicle to manifest and access the desired experience. This player you could call God or The Creator.

- Then we have the machine itself, with the screen ready to be accessed, and the ability to create the experience or reality you want to play in. This can be called The Ether.

- Then we have the switch turned on, and the electricity going through the system, to create the chosen reality and manifest it on the screen. You could call this The Holy Spirit or The Force.

- Then we have the character being created on the screen with attributes like strength, speed, size etc. This could be *you*, the vehicle created for unlimited imagination and to have limited experiences in a chosen reality within the boundaries, laws and creation of that reality – Natural Law.

In this game the powers and attributes of the character are created before the start of the game and he/she/it is ready for action. In real life, as a human being, we are created at conception. Two humans – characters – come together to create another unique one with the strengths and weaknesses of the former two. We are made. We are then born into a world that we – the characters – know nothing about. If we did, life would be boring and have no challenges or surprises.

The next stages of development – up until about six years old – are all about absorbing information from the reality/environment to set that new character up for the rest of the experience in the perceived environment that we call life. At this stage we are still connected and guided by source/spirit and imagination.

Life though is flowing so fast with so much incoming information that we react automatically based on how we were programmed at conception and during the first years of life. Our programmes are where we put meaning on the information so we can react in balance according to our beliefs. We simply could not consciously stop and make a conscious decision for all incoming information as it's so vast and life would not be able to flow. Remember, these are just beliefs which create perceptions of reality and are not truths in themselves.

We absorb these beliefs by observing life around us and how people react to life, mainly from the mother at birth, and as the baby grows, then the father and close family and friends. Then as young children we are exposed to more of our environment and experiences to give us more information about the world we live in. At this age we do not judge, we just absorb life. One simple example would be your reaction to seeing a large spider. Depending on where you were brought up, and how you observed people reacting around spiders, and your own personal experiences as a child, you may put the belief/programme as "dangerous" or "interesting". One belief/programme on seeing a large spider would put you in a state of flight or flight. While the other puts you in a more curious state. You would perceive the situation as fearful or safe. Both are valid – possibly true but not absolute truths – the spider is just a spider. Some spiders may become aggressive when threatened or touched accidently, but mainly they just pass us by without us knowing. It is our own personal experience with them that will create our own personal belief about them. This is a simple example of how we translate the incoming information into daily behaviour.

So the answer to the questions are as follows:

What is life?

Life is movement. An exchange of information from our individual inner world with the outer world. Simple cause and effect. We react to the incoming information of the world just as the world reacts to the information we put out. These reactions cause movement and movement is life. We are aware of this life because we are conscious. Due to memory we are able to process and remember the passing of events and this memory gives us what we perceive as the passing of time. We are also able, through imagination, to create a vision of the future to allow us to plan, hope and dream. The only true reality though is the ever changing *now*. As it is said: "Change is the universal constant". The only thing that never changes is change itself because without change/movement there can be no life.

Where does life come from?

Life comes from a point of possibility outside of existence, time and space that many people call God or The Creator. If forced to define God in one word it would be Imagination. God is all possibility, everything and nothing, all imagination. Life then is the manifestation of the imagination of God. We are literally living in the mind and dreams of God. Our Universe is maybe one creative thought amongst unlimited creative thoughts and therefore unlimited universes. We just happen to be on one planet in one universe run by absolute morons and psychopaths and are having a hard time dealing with it. Maybe it's bad luck, or just maybe, it's an incredible challenge that makes life exciting. I'll let you decide that one.

How does life function?

Life functions through Natural Laws and habits (routines) that seem to have an intelligent purpose integrated within. That purpose we call evolution. A need/urge to move forward, improve, advance and there seems to be clear laws that enable that process.

We are a mind field of consciousness using the physical body as a sensory vehicle to perceive and experience this reality on planet Earth.

PERCEPTION

The linear path of incoming information from the environment, to you reacting to it, is:

Incoming information – perception – programme – behaviour/reaction.

So, if we look at this pathway, and where we can make changes, then it seems clear that perception is the one place we can intervene. The outside environment is mostly out of our control, some things can be changed yes, but apart from moving to a new environment most of it is out of our control. Also, in a world of over 7 billion different people, with 7 billion different views on life, trying to change the outside world to your liking alone will only lead to confrontation and violence. A simple example of that would be the weather. If you want permanent sun then a move to southern Spain may be required. But if you live in the UK, you best get used to the full four seasons and dark skies.

So perception is where we can intervene and this perception is controlled by our subconscious belief programmes. This means it is not really an event or the environment we react to but our perception of it. Knowing this, we realise that by becoming aware we can now decide what meaning we wish to put on that information. Suddenly we can decide a rainy day means joy. We decide it is all part of nature's glory and all weather is to be embraced. Yes, we can really decide that.

The book, *Little Miracle Baby: The Perfect Life of Kennedy Jack* by Patrick Quanten MD, shows that life is not really just about what we see, or are experiencing, but how we perceive it and how we deal with it. Sometimes what we perceive as tragedy can have within it a spiritual message – a much-needed spiritual message.

The book and film, *Into the Wild* by Jon Krakauer, is another example of how one event can be perceived in many ways. After leaving his family, Chris McCandless was found two years or so later dead in the Alaskan wilderness. He died of starvation after some bad luck on what was to be his last adventure. Many writers saw him as reckless, foolish, a bad example to others. Yet some find it a beautiful story of a young man out for adventure and living the life he consciously chose. His last gift to the world was a photo of a young man, clearly very thin, but with a big smile on his face and leaving his last note to the world:

"I have had a happy life and thank the Lord. Goodbye and may God bless all!" – Chris McCandless.

I'm sure his family will be saddened by their loss, but what is the real message in his story? I guess only you can decide that. For Chris himself, it seemed that, although he had no desire to die, he chose to live life to the full with all the risks and dangers and felt blessed for the brief experience on this planet.

Try and be aware, when stressed, what the actual problem is, and if it is really that important, or can it be perceived in another more beneficial or less impacting way?

It has also been shown that cells move towards things they see as nutritious and away from things that are toxic. As an organism of trillions of cells, humans will function in the same way. Again though, the issue is perception.

It is also said that when making decisions we make the decision that brings us the closest to pleasure and the furthest away from pain. That decision making too is based on the belief of the person. Yes, there are clearly things that are very toxic to the human form, regardless of how we perceive them, fire being an obvious example. All clear-thinking humans would try to get out of a house fire and onto the road, getting away from what is toxic, the fire, and towards the nutrition of safety, the road. A heroin addict will continue to take a drug that is slowly killing him/her as it is closer to pleasure than dealing with life as it is. So people can move towards and take something that is clearly toxic and painful because in the perception of themselves and the world it is less toxic and less painful than their perceived reality.

AWARENESS

Awareness of your present state of mind – I will put this into three basic states.

Body and focused mind experience means we are not really aware, and as such, we are in total focus on the physical task in hand. Playing a tennis match requires total focus. At that point in time nothing else exists except the ball, the racket and the opponent. This is being completely in the present moment. But we have to remember not all present moments are fun like playing tennis. Total focus can indeed be great when focusing on a task, especially a fun task, but total focus is also used when we are in danger and feel threatened. We don't worry about the flowers in the jungle and the deer when a tiger leaps out at us. The tiger becomes *all* reality and our fight and flight kicks in and all that matters is survival. We escape and lie under a tree and gradually our system functions as normal again and the world opens up with all it has available. But if we believe we are in constant danger, for example from financial worries, work, relationships, war, viruses and more, we are then on constant alert and massive amounts of energy are drained from our system. So remember, total focus has its use, but at the right time, and for the right reasons.

A conscious body–mind–environment experience means we are going about our normal daily tasks with a good level of awareness of the present task and the outer environment and all that is in it. It's our normal state, which could be called a balanced state, that helps us to do the present task, but also to be able to respond to other information coming in. A great state of flexibility that enables us to go through the day ready for all that comes our way, the good, bad and ugly. We can call this state "healthy detachment".

A detached view of yourself from the "God" perspective. This allows us to step outside of ourselves and observe our own life and reactions to the world we live in. Becoming totally conscious of who we are and the influences on our lives. From this state we can take a break from the pressures of life knowing "it's just a ride". Stopping maybe three times a day to breathe and reflect on our reactions is so important. For one, it allows the stress of the day to cease, allowing the system to be calm. Then it allows us to focus on changing our reactions and thereby breaking the negative patterns controlling us throughout the day.

One great tip to start the day is standing straight, chest out, head high, taking deep breaths and focusing on what you want to achieve that day. When you do this, your whole emotional state will change instantly. This should also be repeated as many times as you can throughout the day, especially when you become aware your emotional state is starting to become negative. Being aware of this before you become overcome by it helps you to snap out of it and to return quickly to a more positive state of mind, thereby enabling you to make more positive decisions. Every time you get angry in the day use the breathing time to go back into a calm state and to see what the trigger was. Was there a genuine reason for your anger or was there something said that triggered an underlying belief of yourself or the world? Try and reflect and ask yourself why you make the decisions you make and what belief systems the decisions are based on. Be honest with yourself especially when you are making a conscious decision. If there is a choice/reaction you have to think about, what is it that drives your choice? Do you make a choice because you think it is the right choice, whether intellectually or morally, or do you make a choice based on fear of consequences or what others may think?

A true free choice means doing what you believe to be morally right regardless of the consequences. If you have to think of the consequences before you make a decision then it cannot be said to be a free choice and true health and balance cannot be achieved. Eventually you are able to just *be* and go about your day knowing and trusting that your instincts will alert you to anything that may disturb your balance.

THE LAW OF ATTRACTION OR THE LAW OF AWARENESS?

Many people talk about the "law of attraction" and how to draw experiences and opportunities into their lives. Although there is something in this, it is something very difficult to prove in a scientific manner. What can be called "the law of awareness" on the other hand is real and simple to explain.

Imagine you are entering a supermarket and the only thing you want to buy is a tin of beans. You go into the store and your mind is already planning your route to the aisle with the tins of beans. You walk up and down maybe three or four aisles and pass maybe fifty people and then you reach your destination, the tins of beans. You pick one up and go straight to the check-out, pay and walk right back to your car and back home. The only thing on your mind was the tin of beans and the only experience you had was finding and buying the tin of beans.

But if you were to stop at the moment when you make eye contact with the tin of beans and are about to pick it up you would notice that that is all you would see. Zoom out a little and you would see tins of soup, maybe some pasta. Zoom out some more and there would be the freezer section, the bakery, the wine section and what the entire store has to offer. You only saw the beans because that was your total focus and the only experience you were looking for. Zooming right out, there may have been friends in the store, special offers, a job vacancy, some free samples and much more. If you had entered the store in a more open and aware state you would have seen all those things and still got your tin of beans. Energy goes where attention flows.

Now imagine sitting on a sunny day on the promenade in Penzance, Cornwall, or at any other beachside town. Around you are masses of people. Groups of youngsters skate boarding, families strolling in the sun enjoying an ice-cream, small fishing boats leaving Newlyn harbour for a day's fishing or even the bigger boats out for the week. Then the local seal pops his head up to gaze at the strange creatures on the shore. Maybe in the distance a pod of dolphins is making a fleeting visit and playing around the gig boats out for a day's rowing. Sitting on a bench are two middle-aged men, clearly having had one too many beers, having an argument. You may see litter or you may see flowers. All life is around you, the good, the bad and the ugly. What tends to happen though is people see what they are looking for, and on many occasions, unconsciously looking for. Out of all that is around you, what do you see? What do you focus on?

As you are walking home, are you thinking about your glimpse of nature in the sea, the beauty of families together and strolling in the sun, or the two drunks arguing on the bench? Did you see all there was to see or just one of the many possible sights? Did your perception of life and your focus limit you to one thing and therefore gave you one view of life on Penzance Prom? Did you feel blessed for seeing the dolphins or depressed for seeing the drunks? With all of life, all around us, all the time, it seems we can choose where we focus our attention and therefore how we feel about life itself. In cell cultures, cells are attracted to nutrition and turn away from toxicity. In life we do the same, only life is full of everything which can be perceived as toxic or nutritious for the individual. By becoming aware of what is nutritious to us as individuals and by focusing on just that in our environment we can find what we need to help us grow and develop. We may not be able to escape what we do not like, but we can make an effort and simply not engage.

The same can be said of our perceptions and relationships with partners, friends, work colleagues and family. Most of us have what could be perceived as good as well as annoying qualities. There may be some people that are bad through and through, and even less fully good, but most of us are a collection of all things. We tend, though, to focus on the qualities we really like in other people and miss the ones we don't like. Or we constantly get angry at the things we don't like whilst missing the kind qualities. Try and observe people as they really are as a whole in order to gain a full rounded opinion of them and to develop your relationships from there.

In life, especially in the manufactured rat race, we have little free time and we tend to be very focused on small things and rushing to get things done. We may go home tired and then start to complain about our jobs, relationships, lack of free time and lack of opportunity. But it is quite easy to imagine that every day we pass up on masses of opportunities simply because we are not open to anything new that may arise.

The law of attraction states that by changing our emotional state we draw in things to mirror that emotional state. This could well be true but very difficult to provide any real hard evidence of this. The law of awareness states that a multitude of experiences and opportunities are always there but we simply walk past them every day as we are not open to them and our focus is on perpetuating and surviving the conveyor belt of madness. If you believe the world is a hard, lonely, unforgiving place then you will see things in your life that reflect that message even though many other things that show beauty, compassion and joy are present at the same time. Try and decide what experiences you want and how to open up to them. Look for the beauty in life and nurture yourself with the opportunity to learn, grow and become fulfilled. You can even try different days going out with a different thing to focus on and see how much you notice it in your day as opposed to other days when your focus was elsewhere. This shows us there is plenty of information and opportunity every day in our lives if we open up to it. Choose to find the information and experiences that build you up instead of the information and experiences that drag you down.

"The Law of Attraction requires Action". This is the step most people fail at. Getting off their backside and putting things into action. It's all well and good gaining self-knowledge, awareness of the world, and seeing your true goals, but nothing will change unless *you* make it change. If it is fear that holds you back, just take a deep breath and do it anyway. It's a bit like going for a swim in the Atlantic without a wet-suit. Just dive in. Yes, it will be cold and uncomfortable for a minute or so, but after that the body warms up, the mind clears, and you get the real feeling of being alive. But you have to jump in first and only you can do that.

If you think of all individual aspects of life as having their own living energy field, by focusing on what you want, and want to achieve, you are then feeding that energy field. In the same manner that the Cherokee elder told his grandson of the tale of the battle of the two wolves within, one was evil and one was good. The boy asked, "Which one wins?" The elder responded, "The one you feed". So by also putting positive energy into the external things we want and ideas we want to manifest, we can feed their energy fields too. To do this we first need to be aware of what we truly want. Then whether we attract that into our lives, or whether we simply feed the energy field of that reality with our attention, it doesn't really matter. What matters is what positive things we are trying to create in our lives. It is good to be aware of the negative things going on around us so we can avoid being involved in bad experiences, but a constant focus of the negative will in the end feed that reality, and lock us away from other experiences available to us in the same moment, experiences that could build us up.

These concentric circles represent where your focus is in relation to all the information in the environment. The centre is your total attention on one thing. This is all you are aware of in that moment. The more you expand your awareness the more information and possibilities come into your life.

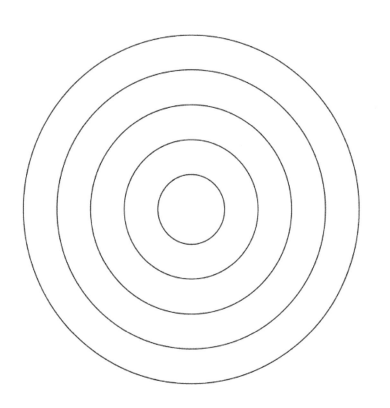

CLARITY

"It is indeed simple. Energy creates matter. Matter is a condensation of energy. Mind has no matter and is therefore simple energy. Matter comes later. One may say, matter is formed through the mind, and functions through the mind. What happens with consciousness and specifically with the conscious mind? The senses open up the conscious mind. It is the information picked through the senses that will make us aware of the environment, of the reality, but seen in a specific way and that is the way the brain, the nervous system, interprets the incoming information. The brain plays an important part in the conscious mind. It plays no part in the mind itself. The conscious mind works through the matter and is linked to the brain function. The mind is an energy field that just is. The conscious mind is intrinsically linked to an individual. The mind exists without a body".*

– Patrick Quanten

So there we have the relationship between the mind and the brain. The issue with modern life is that the brain is picking up so much information and our focus always seems to be on getting things done and rushing about. We never have time to settle down and just be.

Think of the example of the snow-globe, a popular souvenir found in many gift shops. You shake the globe and the mass of snow now clouds the view. It is not clear exactly what is to be seen behind the snowfall. This seems to be a good illustration of how we are living our lives and the state of our minds. There's far too much going on to see clearly. To actually see clearly the view on display in the snow-globe, we have to put it down and leave it alone, so it becomes still. To bring some clarity to our lives and to try to figure out why things are so hectic and tiring and out of balance, to see the picture of life in front of us, we just need to stop. Not actually do something about the problem, but actually just stop. Stopping means not just a physical act, but also to stop trying to think our way out of a problem when in fact we are just throwing more snow into the globe and shaking it about even more. Stopping means also stopping to think. A tried and tested way of doing this is fasting.

Taking three days out of your life to just let the mind and body settle is the equivalent of just putting the snow-globe down and letting it settle all by itself, so the clear picture can reveal itself without any effort at all on our part. To start to understand the world, and our own role in life and in human existence, we first need the mental clarity to try to see the world as it really is and not how our busy lives or other unknown sources are telling us it is. Clarity helps us to start again with a blank page and to try and see the world as it is and what it is trying to tell us. In a world where most of us are looking to find who we really are, maybe a better way would be to throw away what we are not and see what is left. To find a needle in a haystack, it is best to throw away all the hay, and what is left must be the needle, rather than to throw the hay about randomly looking for a needle.

When we put all these factors together, we see that a balance of who we are, how we are made, the life we want to live, and the environment, is what is needed to maintain health. Maintaining a stable internal equilibrium in a constantly changing external environment, whilst performing all of the functions necessary for life, is called *homeostasis*. Sometimes though, life brings us challenges, whether physical, emotional, environmental or whatever. These challenges mean we need to be flexible to life, to the changing situations in the environment, and to our own inner world. Challenges give the individual an opportunity to grow, learn and evolve.

In his book, *The Science of Health and Healing*, Trevor Gunn gives four possible outcomes to the challenges that we call illness. These outcomes can be used in what we call physical, emotional or psychological illness. It seems clear then that we have to process information, especially toxic information, in a way it can be dealt with and cleared out by the system. If that clear-out is suppressed, which is the basis for allopathic medicine, it will only accumulate in the system and cause bigger issues. No different really from not taking out the rubbish in your house on a regular basis.

- The individual resolves the illness and as a result their health is improved and they are stronger than they were before. They are less susceptible to those problems after the illness and more able to deal with them.

- The individual resolves the illness but there has been no learning as such. They are not stronger than they were before. They effectively carry on as they were before the illness, just as susceptible to succumbing to the illness as they were before.

- The illness is not resolved and as a result the health of the individual is worse than before and they descend into a lower level of chronic illness, more susceptible than before.

- The illness is not resolved and the individual is unable to react sufficiently to overcome the problem and dies.

It seems mankind, for a long time, has being going, and has been driven, into a lower level of chronic illness, physically and psychologically. We are at the point of being totally dependent on external "experts" to tell us who we are and why we are ill. The more we give power away to these "experts" the more we detach from the wisdom that created us and sustains us and from the knowing that will bring balance and health back to our lives.

ACKNOWLEDGING THE MONSTER WITHIN

When taking a look at tyrants in the recent past like Stalin, Mao and Hitler, the vast majority of people will be appalled and shocked at how human beings can behave in such a cold and callous way. For most people it is beyond their imagination the horrors these people inflicted, and again, the vast majority would clearly state they could not and would not be able to commit such atrocities. But the disturbing fact is that the majority of the population supported these regimes.

In Nazi Germany, Hitler and his ethnic cleansing had the majority support of the people. The infamous words of Professor Jordan Peterson, *"You probably would have been a Nazi too"*, are completely backed up with the actual reality of what happened. A look at the last two years around the world, and history is clearly, for those who can see, repeating itself. Hundreds of millions of people in the west locked down by the orders of one leader in each country. The vast majority of people obediently went home and ceased to live until further notice. The rebels who decided that the requirements of life still needed to be provided for and carried on as normal, were hounded, beaten, imprisoned, and fined by the police and ratted on by their friends and neighbours. All of this done by people thinking they were doing the right thing, or simply not thinking at all, and just following orders. It seems history does repeat itself, especially if no lessons were learnt.

The truth is that in certain circumstances, people with certain beliefs, creating certain perceptions, can commit all manner of atrocities without even knowing.

Are we meant to believe that these tyrants just sat down one day and decided to create a dictatorship and slaughter millions of innocent people? Are we meant to believe they consciously knew what they were doing?

To even begin to judge these people, we really need to take a look into how a belief can completely take over a person and create a totally rigid way of thinking – a way of thinking that tells them they are right. So anybody who does not agree, not only must be wrong, but must be the enemy, and an enemy of what is right.

We can think of a belief as an energy field, a living energy field, occupying a space in our mind, or our mind-field. Like all living entities it wants to feed itself and grow. A belief can do this by making the person perceive the world and events in a certain way, a way that will feed and help the energy field of that belief to grow. This in turn creates a more rigid perception of the world and again allows the belief to grow. When a belief has grown to such an extent that there can be no space for other views, the individual becomes totally mind controlled by the said belief. We are all built the same and so all have the potential to become totally dominated by a belief.

The vast majority of people, who supported the atrocities of the past centuries, would have done so unknowingly and would have been controlled by a belief and a perception put there by the charismatic dictators. The dictators themselves then get feedback from the people and this in turn gets fed back to the people and this exchange continues until the force of this belief is all powerful and all dominant. There is a huge element of this in the present time that is being consciously manipulated by people in suits behind desks in closed rooms and we will cover this later. There is also the element of people going along with it because of fear of the consequences if they don't, whether ridicule or government punishment.

The way to avoid becoming the monster is to acknowledge the monster within. Acknowledge it as a possibility under a given circumstance, and acknowledge that, unless kept under control, it could be unleashed on your family, friends or even the entire world. This monster does not have to be a tyrant against all of humanity, but could simply be a tyrant against your partner, your children, or simply people you dislike.

The awareness of this stops you being "a Nazi too". The people it seems who are most susceptible in allowing this monster to grow are the people who perceive themselves as nice and virtuous and this naivety makes them totally unaware of the monster when it's unleashed. Being nice is also useless in stopping the monster if it is unleashed in your country or community.

A strong "*no*" with serious intentions beats nice anytime.

HEALTH AND FREEDOM

We all want to be healthy. And we all want to be free. To believe we are healthy, to believe we are free, is not good enough as, somehow, we realise that "believing" is not reality. We believe we live healthy lives right up to the moment we become ill, which illustrates quite clearly that our lives can't have been healthy as it has led to illness. In the same way we believe we live free lives right up to the point we are confronted with the reality that we are not "allowed" to make our own decisions. As long as we believe, we are happy, not necessarily healthy and free, but just happy.

Happiness is a state of mind we put ourselves into, regardless of the reality of our lives. The confrontation with that reality then makes us unhappy and we are looking for someone or something to blame. It can't be me, as I was happy before, so I cannot have created my unhappiness. The truth is that being happy is a state of mind, which means that being unhappy is also a state of mind. One we put ourselves into. However, we are not inclined to take responsibility for that! We find it extremely hard to admit that we are the sole cause of our unhappiness.

If we no longer want to live in a fake belief system then we need to find out what the reality of health and freedom truly contains. Even doctors will tell you that it isn't because you feel well that you are healthy. They want us to be afraid of diseases we "cannot feel", diseases that have no symptoms until it is too late. Luckily for us, they claim that they can excavate those diseases for us, tell us whether or not we are going to become ill. However, those same doctors have told a myriad of people that they were healthy, that there was nothing to worry about, only for these people to drop dead overnight.

Taking note of both observations, one can question what it truly is these doctors think they know, and how much does what they think they know, relate to the reality of life. Do you want to continue relying on their opinion about your health?

Health has been described in ancient health systems and philosophies as *an imbalance*. When life gets pushed sideways it becomes more and more difficult to maintain your balance in life and eventually you will "fall over". Your system will no longer be able to maintain a normal function. You are clearly ill.

What imbalance are they talking about? Well, it is the individual who becomes ill and has been pushed out of balance. Hence, they are talking about an individual balance. It is the balance that the individual requires in life that will keep him/her functioning properly and easily. But as we know, all of us are different in so many aspects as human beings. We are all humans. We have that in common. But at the same time there are an enormous number of aspects that are completely different, some are even the total opposite. A person born and raised, from local parents, in the northern regions of our planet will, inherently, have a protection against the cold environment and will be warm at temperatures at the lower end of the scale. In contrast, a person from the equator will have a natural protection against the heat and will be comfortable in relatively high temperatures. These kinds of differences between how people comfortably function can be found in all aspects of life.

So "the balance" of life, what is required to maintain an easy life, is different for different people. The truth is that even within small communities every individual has slightly different needs. Take a look at how your neighbours live their lives, what their priorities are, what choices they make, and notice how these are different from your own. Each individual has a need for a different balance in life in order to function easily, in order to be healthy. Hence, health, the inner balance, has a direct relationship with its outer environment. The inner balance of a person depends on the interaction of that person with his/her environment. The more elements that are crucial to the individual and that are being met by the environment at any given moment in time, the easier it will be for that individual to remain in balance, to remain healthy.

As the environment is constantly on the move, constantly changing – simply consider the weather as an example – the individual, ideally, needs to adjust to these changes constantly. Each individual, therefore, comes into this world with a natural range of adjustability. Although your inner metabolism functions optimally at 37°C you will still be alive at 35°C or at 41°C. (These are not the absolute limits of our body temperature; they are simply illustrations of the range.) So, inherently the body naturally adjusts to whatever makes life a little easier, taking its clues from our environment and relating that to the inner needs of the individual. There are limits as to how far a specific individual can "bend" to make these adjustments before it "snaps", but within those boundaries of its construction, nature will automatically adjust.

So there are a few important points we need to remember here.

1. Life is about maintaining an inner balance.

2. An individual life depends on a balance between the individual and his/her environment.

3. Maintaining such a balance happens automatically.

4. Each individual has a unique setting to meet the outside living conditions.

5. Each individual has a unique response to the outside living conditions.

6. Each individual has unique limitations in his/her response to the outside living conditions.

Health, for each individual, means maintaining an ever-changing balance between his/her inner requirements and what the environment has to offer. It all happens automatically. We do not need to work at our health. And that is why babies survive! They naturally do what they need to do, both internally and by sending appropriate messages into their outer world. All of it is a natural process, an automated "conversation" between inner and outer world, a constant exchange of information. And the adjustment to maintain the inner balance, to maintain health, is made by the individual and happens internally. The environment is what it is, and the individual adjusts to it, as best as he/she can. The effect on that inner balance then depends on the limits on which that particular life has been built and the specific tools that particular life came into the world with. Everybody is different in how well they are able to adjust to the given circumstances of the environment at any given moment in time. No two adjustments are exactly the same.

If whatever adjustment the individual has to make falls outside the reach and outside of the limits of that specific life, then that individual will cease to exist. Death occurs when the organism is no longer capable of making the required adjustment to maintain functioning within the outside living conditions as they are. Death is a natural part of life. Life can never be extended beyond the limitations that the individual organism has, with which he/she is able to maintain its own balance in life.

Not only do the external conditions alter continuously, the inner needs for the individual change also. Growing up from baby into adulthood clearly shows us how our inner needs change and how the system automatically adjusts to the development stage it finds itself in. And it doesn't stop there; as we grow older our needs in life keep changing. Different stages in life mean different pressures on different parts of the structure. It is for this reason that the system sheds part of the structure it no longer needs and rebuilds some of its structure in order to cope with its changing position within its environment. As an adult we have more responsibilities, more things "to take care of" than when we were toddlers. Hence, our system needs to be able to cope with these changing requirements and therefore needs to change. Again, we do not need to work at it. It simply happens, just as it needs to.

So we have a constantly changing inner environment, surrounded by a constantly changing outer environment, both of which are maintaining a natural balance for themselves. Nature, as we define it as our living outside environment, is constantly responding to changing inner stimuli, stimuli within nature itself. Whatever happens in nature, there will always be a response from nature that will restore a balance in which nature itself can continue living.

Life may have changed, but it continues, which means that nature is able to adjust its balance in order to continue its journey through life, its life. Nature is still functioning within its set limitations, and don't worry, it hasn't reached the end of its life cycle yet, not by a long way.

A similar system operates within each organism. Whatever changes inside, irrespective of where those changes originated from, the organism, the individual, will naturally respond, adjust, within its own limitations, using its own capabilities and tools. Inside all of us lies a natural system that knows how to adjust in order to continue living. Life may have changed but it continues. Our own "nature" knows what to do. Luckily for us, we do not need to know. We do not have to make those kinds of decisions. We do not have to work at it. The only thing that is required is that our system has maximum freedom to execute what it knows it needs to do.

In order for our system to maintain its own balance to the best of its capability, it requires the freedom to do what it needs to do. Seems simple enough, as all animals and all plants do it all the time. And yet, this is where us human beings have the problem. We reason. We "invent" logic. We become obsessed with our thinking skills. We think we know better. We think we have "discovered" lots of things about life itself. We think we know what to do in order to achieve a specific result, to manipulate things to our advantage. And yet, this is exactly where we show our stupidity! Even when we observe that the specific effect we are after is not being achieved by our decisions and actions we still continue to believe that we are right. Life is showing us the reality, and we still choose a belief system, an illusion. We remain stubbornly hooked on our belief, Pride and stubbornness.

One important reason why we are confronted by the failure to achieve the specific outcome we crave is because we believe that *what we think is right* must be right for everybody, and must be right in all circumstances. We are trying to squeeze individual lives and individual balances into generalized statements and general styles of living – so called for the common good. What we declare to be "beneficial" for the majority of people (how do you measure benefit?) must be used by everyone. It becomes "the standard" in human life. It gets the seal of approval, and without that seal, one is on shaky ground, apparently.

We have, however, lost sight of who is telling us what is beneficial, and what must be the standard. In nature, it is the individual who, unconsciously, assesses the situation and responds, unconsciously, to it. In what has been called "our modern society", someone has taken it upon themselves to declare what is beneficial to all. The individual's observations, analyses and responses have been dismissed as amateur and dangerous. We have allowed other human beings to take over the evaluation of our individual life, to take over nature itself. We have come so far that some specialist human beings actually declare that nature makes mistakes and that human beings need to take over if we want to survive as a species, or even as an earth. This implies that we human beings know better than nature, even though nature has been around for 13.4 billion years, according to human calculations. Also completely forgetting that human beings are *part* of nature – created by nature – not the other way around. Nature is the greater power and human beings are only a very small part within the larger picture. What is the problem then? How did it come to this imbalanced view of life?

The problem is human consciousness. The human part of creation is to become aware of what there is we need to learn, what is truly there and how it functions. The role of humanity within creation is to make creation become aware of itself. So we can think for ourselves and we will be learning, at a conscious level, what we as natural organisms already know.

So, unlike any other part of creation, the human being thinks. And because this is the main path of our development, we use it all the time and we attach enormous value to it. Right from the beginning, long before we really "know" anything. Hence, we think we know better. By injecting what we think we know into our lives, by insisting every human being follows the instructions of what some human beings *think* they know, we override the responses of every individual by implementing something else. This something else differs from what nature naturally wants to do, how it naturally wants to respond, and therefore this something else is always restricting and limiting what nature is "allowed" to do. As a result, many internal responses to changing circumstances are inadequate and life continues with the system being out of balance and remaining out of balance. If it isn't allowed to execute what it absolutely requires for that individual to balance his/her life, then that individual will continue to live out of balance, in effect being ill. And we do get signs and signals about this imbalance, but human beings, who know better, are doing everything they can to cover up those signs and signals in order for us to believe we are healthy and in balance. They have their reputation to think about. They have built their lives on guiding others, on overriding natural tendencies in other individuals, and they are very reluctant to give up that power.

The main point here, however, is that in order for the natural system of a human being to function optimally, to be able to maintain a balance in life, it must have the freedom to do so. This means that every individual must be allowed to respond to whatever living circumstances he/she finds themselves in without any restrictions by other human beings. An individual should have the freedom to respond as one natural system to another and as one natural system to its inner changes. This means that not only should a public healthcare system *not* exist, but also, that virtually no other social restrictions on individual behaviour should be implemented either. We should be truly free!

Okay, I'll stop here, before you end up with a heart attack imagining the chaos and lawlessness of human society when we allow every single individual to do whatever he or she wants to do. A free for all is not what I am advocating here, but I will return to this later on. What is important, however, is noticing what point we have reached by analysing life itself. We were looking for answers as to what health is, and how it can be achieved, and we ended up in the knowledge that health is an individual matter and that health requires total individual freedom. Health and freedom are irrevocably linked together, which means that *disease is an expression of restricted freedom.* Whenever an individual becomes imprisoned, enslaved, restricted, he or she is on their way to ill-health. Disease is the natural and unavoidable result of non-freedom for the individual. Not being allowed to live life the way nature intended will make the individual ill, and if one lives in a society where individual freedom has been banned, the predictable outcome is for this society, as a whole, to be diseased.

FREE WILL

Human society is littered with the word freedom. We have the fight for freedom, the right to freedom, and the notion that only freedom must be acceptable. And yet, the structure of human society, in its different forms, does not seem to express the definition of freedom. The definition is quite clear: *the power or right to act, speak or think as one wants*. Or one can put it differently: *the state of not being imprisoned or enslaved*. Going by these definitions of freedom, no human society allows freedom for its population.

This, at least, must be clear. There are rules everywhere that one needs to adhere to and there is punishment when one doesn't. In spite of this, we vehemently believe we live in a free society and we criticize other societies, "rival" societies, for not allowing the freedom we perceive we have. So what we believe seems to be completely dissociated from the reality of our lives, but we fail to see it or acknowledge it. Freedom seems to be more of a perception than it is a reality.

In our drive to want to be free we make the association to having a free will. Willing to be free has been put at the same level as having a free will. The two are, in our belief, intrinsically linked. We have argued that in order to have a real opportunity to be healthy, we need the freedom to have our own feelings, thoughts and actions, which is exactly what the definition of freedom says. So a free will, the ability to make and act upon your own decisions, is an essential part of life for every individual, or so it seems. To make up your own mind and to decide for yourself what to do is fundamental, not only to a free life, but to a healthy life. So can this free will be found anywhere?

Let's have a look at the structure of life first before we analyse how life functions. Each species within creation occupies a specific part of the spectrum of the entire manifestation of the physical world. It cannot move beyond the boundaries of the bandwidth it is "imprisoned" in. So the part of the spectrum that manifests as plant life is completely separate from that of the invertebrates, and these are separate from the vertebrates. Within the separate bands of the spectrum; each species occupies a well-defined space and there cannot be any exceptions to this. So within the band of the mammals (part of the vertebrates), the manifestation of the dog is in a totally different place on the spectrum than that of an elephant or a monkey. Each species is the expression of a "fixed" frequency within the bandwidth that manifests the mammals. Each species therefore is completely recognisable and has distinct features that cannot be confused with other species.

A further division shows us that within each species group there are several sub-groups, again with distinct features that separates them from the others. Each time we identify distinct features we are looking at a different part of the energy spectrum that has been fixed into matter. It is no different for humanity. Humanity is a distinctly different group amongst mammals. It cannot be confused with other mammals because it is the manifestation of a different frequency within the band that produces mammals. Within the human race there are distinctly different races to be identified, whereby humans from the same race share some characteristics that are not or differently present in other groups. This also is an expression of the fixation of different frequencies within the bandwidth that produces humans. Having characteristics of a specific human race "binds" you to that race. You cannot change the characteristics. You cannot change the frequency in which your life has been fixed.

Within every race there are a large number of individuals. Each one being slightly different from the next, even though they can be identified as belonging to a certain bandwidth, or certain race, within humanity, which in turn, is the manifestation of a specific bandwidth of frequencies. Hence, each life has unique qualities that are an expression of a very narrow band, call it a frequency, within the spectrum of creation. That individual life is "fixed", is stuck with those characteristics and fits perfectly in one specific place of the spectrum. It has its boundaries and cannot move beyond them as a physically present living organism. The entire human spectrum, across the various races, is expressed in individual entities of that spectrum, each representing one human being. This means that you cannot be anybody else than the person you are. There is freedom for you!

One is stuck in a specific life, with the characteristics of a specific human being, with others occupying different fragments of the human energy field spectrum. And one cannot do anything else but to live the life that your specific expression has been made for. You are the expression of that tiny bit of the energy spectrum of the entire human field, and this expression is also time related. The entire spectrum of the universal energy field, including all of the physical creation, is constantly moving in and out of manifestation and evolving through the influences that every part of the field has on every other part. So the structure of living organisms is fixed within a narrow band of possibilities. While the entire spectrum is moving constantly and changing constantly this material structure of a living organism, which is also true for every human being, remains fixed in its possibilities and its potential. So how can this organism live in a constantly changing environment?

When we examine life in nature and we look at how the living entity comes into being and survives in the outside world, we soon notice a couple of important things. Newly born specimens are not the same. They display different characteristics and reaction patterns already. Scientists have been able to relate some of those characteristics as being an expression of the genetic code of the individual, which has inherited features from previous generations. In other words, every individual has been put together in a slightly different way, which already at birth makes us different from one another. If we are constructed in different ways, all within the human spectrum, then it makes sense that we also, right from the beginning, will act differently. We will have our own peculiar likes and dislikes, no matter how new we are to this life.

Now each of these "different" characters are placed in different environments. This means that people who grow up in different surroundings, where the way people live is not at all the same, they'll have different stimulations and different teachings from the adults they are surrounded with, and generally from the different natural world they are surrounded with. So no wonder they grow up in a different way, once again becoming totally different people, with actions, thoughts and feelings that do not match those of people elsewhere. People that grow up in very similar circumstances will also become different people because they did not have the same characteristics from birth onwards. This means that they respond to similar circumstances differently, thereby enlarging the differences that already existed between them. What one individual likes and responds to by pursuing it will be disliked by another, and hated by a third. They all respond differently to their environment which is beginning to shape all of their lives. These responses are intuitive, meaning devoid of any reasoning. These responses are driven by natural forces and are the result of these forces, along with inner and outer "circumstances". This mechanism is not showing any signs of a free will of the individual. They learn how to survive in a way that is best suited to how they have been constructed and what they have learned in the early confrontations with their environment. Learning how to survive is learning reaction patterns that automatically protect you from getting hurt or from being pushed out. And how one has learned to respond to a given situation is not how another does it. The way any organism, including human beings, functions, the way they have learned to survive, has become an automated response to the stimuli of an ever-changing world, inside and outside of the organism. It knows what is best and it does it. So no free will there either!

For these survival mechanisms to work properly they have to become automatic and instantaneous. No more consulting.

No more pros and cons. Just instant unconscious reacting, so you can save energy for other things. Every individual now has become an automated response machine, based on the individual construction and on the individual schooling the person has received. Every individual operates from an unconscious database which has basic layout features that are different for each individual, and different information stored, because of different experiences each individual has had. Each of us is locked into a set of behavioural patterns that run our lives for us, patterns we are not even conscious of. There is freedom for you!

Nature has everything pre-programmed and functions on an action-reaction basis. If we observe the natural world, we can see that every living organism responds to a given situation in an automatic, intuitive fashion, based on the characteristics of the organism and what it has learned from earlier encounters with its environment. Knowing these two factors allows you to accurately predict the outcome of every interaction in nature. Of course, you do have to truly know all of these factors, while most of the time we pretend to know and then we are surprised when something else occurs unexpectedly. That "unexpectedly" is proof of our ignorance, not proof that there are exceptions in nature. There exists none. It all happens as a result of interactions that are built in within the structure of nature and that are following the path of evolution, of a developing nature and a developing universe.

And then human beings come along and they demand "home ruling". They demand free will. Who are they demanding it from? They want to be free. Free from what? We have just learned that you cannot be free from the restraints of your own life. Nature happens as an action-reaction mechanism between the environment and the individual and vice versa, in patterns that are unconscious and automatic. To any situation you find yourself in you respond. However, you can only choose from the set number of responses that you have in your arsenal. Some you have been given by your family and some you yourself have gathered on the way. That is your personal range of responses. You cannot do anything else. If it were possible in nature for you to respond in a way that is not possible for your system, you'd die, and that is something that your natural system will not allow. It has been created to keep itself alive for as long as possible, given the circumstances it comes across in life.

The demand for a free will originates in our conscious mind, while life happens in, is steered by, and controlled by, our unconscious mind. Free will can only apply within all the limitations that every single life possesses. And ultimately, nature, of which – I cannot emphasize this enough, – we are an *integral part* of, will find the path of least resistance, the path that keeps us alive, even in spite of ourselves. Hence, you could argue that no matter what you "freely" decide in your life you will always end up where your life is supposed to be, as your unconscious mind is in control of your life, not your free will. This is the case because you are a fixed manifestation of a frequency within an entire spectrum, a spectrum that is on the way to somewhere, a spectrum that is in full development from a starting point following a predictable pathway of developmental stages going to a very specific end point. All the points of the entire spectrum move in a very coordinated fashion, and all points evolve over time in a harmonious way. So how can, within such a system, one frequency be allowed to wander off in any direction it chooses, without knowing at all what the complete picture is about?

Outside the boundaries of your life, you do not have any say whatsoever. Inside the boundaries you can choose, but remember that you are programmed, even if your conscious mind does not want to acknowledge this. Your unconscious automatic response comes from somewhere, and it isn't from you making a conscious decision.

So what is then left of my free will?

To put it nicely, one could say that, in terms of the natural world, you are free to choose a path, but whichever path you choose, you will end up in the same place. As an old saying goes, you cannot escape your destiny. This remains true even if you do not believe in destiny. Nature doesn't care about what you think. It will go where it is supposed to go and it knows the easiest route to take you there too. Any decision you make that deviates from this schedule makes the journey more hazardous. Your tiny conscious mind is trying to impose its will upon the unconscious mind, who has the benefit of seeing the larger picture and of overseeing the long-term effects of every possible path in front of you. Your unconscious mind also knows where it is all leading to and what comes next. Your free will can only lead to more suffering as you are trying to force your life to go into a direction it cannot go. If your conscious decisions do allow your life to move on without too many obstacles, without too much resistance, then that means that you are more or less on your natural path, maintaining your natural balance, or put differently, you are on the road your unconscious mind has laid out for you. In other words, you are free to choose what you are meant to do!

Having said all of this, human beings are different from any other species that precedes them in creation. They have what we like to describe as an independent mind. This mind has the ability to construct its own reality. In the entire creation, only humans *believe* things to be true. For all other living creatures there is only one truth and that is what it is and how it is. Human beings then go: "Yes, but …" This is the difference. This is the problem. And this is also our main task within the evolutionary process. We need to learn to match what we believe to the truth.

In the meantime, this human mind has created a human world inside the natural world. This human world has a structure which is not controlled by nature. It is a construction within the natural world, and therefore it cannot escape it, as we have seen before. Humanity is fixed within the energetic field of creation and within that field groups of human beings have created structures for them to live together.

In contrast with nature, where we originate from and what shapes our lives, these structures are mainly built on reasoning, on logic. These are a manifestation of our conscious mind, where reasoning reigns. Our conscious mind, however, is also the place where our imagination fuels a virtual reality. It is where we construct our ideas, based on what we believe rather than on reality. In nature, all interactions are following natural laws. In society, all interactions follow human law, a vision of life that has been constructed on how some of us believe life should be. Here the free will of the individual is restricted by the will of the group, whether the belief is a common belief or whether they are imposed restrictions of a regime, a dominating order that forces everybody under their command to think and act as they are told.

Let's summarize this.

An individual is locked into two very different systems. One is nature, which is in evolution far beyond and above any human will or desire, and the other is a human society, created by a few human beings to serve a few human beings. Neither allows for free individual thought, free individual speech, and free individual action. And yet, every individual has a choice. Or so it seems.

What kind of choice do we have and what is its function?

Our natural path we cannot alter. This means that you have the choice to willingly follow this path or to resist it. As we are biologically locked into the natural system we cannot alter the path, so ultimately what needs to happen will happen. Here, so it seems, our choice is to follow the path of our life, the path of least resistance, or to oppose it, which will result in a lot of pain and hardship that will not actually change anything or get us anywhere different from where our life is going. The construction of nature is finite and its evolvement and growth is predetermined by the seed the entire creation comes from.

The construction of human society is the result of a human consciousness, which creates a world as it is believed to be. What to some individuals appears to be beneficial will be enforced upon an entire group of people, including those that have minds that believe life to be something else. So here we can definitely see that there is room for improvement, room for change. Humanity is in its development at an infant stage and so what the infant believes to be true will change as it grows up and learns more. One infant pretending, believing, to know how it should be done and imposing this upon its peers seems like a cruel and unjust act, which of course it is. For humanity, and consequently the structures it builds, to evolve and grow it needs to expand the mind. It needs to allow the illusionary world of their make-believe to change, to grow, as it learns more and more about the true reality of life. A child needs to grow up, which involves getting to know more about life itself, and consequently altering its beliefs about life. If humanity doesn't allow this natural growth process, then the imaginary picture will clash more and more with the natural system, which results in humans understanding less and less of what is happening to them. They believe they are doing everything right and yet nothing is going right. If you believe that eating sugars makes you fat, and you decide not to eat any more sugars, you expect to be lean and thin, not obese. If, however, you are still obese, you become even more obese (as an individual or as a nation), then you need the freedom to change your mind on what your conscious mind has implemented. You need the free will to change direction in life. Nature won't oppose this, as it already was wondering what the hell you were doing by refusing a necessary asset to life itself, but a society that has created the illusion for its own benefit will resist you wanting to change direction. If you are not complying with the rules of a society, you become a direct threat to the structure of that society. A society only works when the people in it follow the same path. Nature only works when all organisms follow their intended path. The difference is that we are created by nature and therefore have no choice but to follow that path. Human society has not been created by nature, nor has it been created by myself, which are the only two possible ways it could serve me as an individual. As it has been created by another individual it may well suit that individual very well, but maybe

I will need something different for my life to continue with ease. And it is precisely for this reason that a society restricts or even denies any personal choices. Our free will, which is a conscious feature, and therefore does not involve the path of our unconscious mind, our natural way of being, it follows, has a role to play within the conscious part of our lives. This is about what we know and that expresses itself, amongst other ways, in the way we construct how we live together. We can only build something based on what we know, combined with our imagination, which is the part that creates the world that we believe in. It is this interaction that will allow humanity "to move on". However, for this to truly take place humanity needs to let go of what it vehemently holds on to. Society, and human knowledge, can only expand if and when it is prepared to make the necessary changes, to allow different opinions to be evaluated.

People who have created a format of living together in a specific way, giving people rules to live by, have made choices that benefits them. It is by convincing the others that this is a good and beneficial system, that a society is able to form itself. In a way, it is voluntary submission to someone else's rules. Once we voluntarily have done this, these rules can be implemented. Punishment for breaking the rules becomes an accepted feature as fear has taken hold of the group, that, without these rules, the structure will collapse and life will end. Remember that society is built upon one belief of how life is and people cannot "imagine" it to be anything different. If you have grown up in a mafia world then you believe that that is the way the whole world functions. You are likely to be afraid that when the structure falls apart, your life will end too, that it will be crushed underneath the debris of the collapsing structure. You are unable to "imagine" life continuing in a different way.

And yet, at the end of its lifetime, every old structure, made by humans, is bound to perish. Nature will also come to its natural end point, the point where the full potential has been reached. For human structures this end point is reached a lot sooner than it is for nature, as human constructions can only take into account what we know, and that turns out to be very little. Hence, soon the structure reveals its faults and shortcomings and it is then time to replace it with another structure that includes newly gained insights.

It is in this process that humans require a free will, the "right" to be free in thought, speech and action. It is an essential tool for humanity to evolve and to expand its conscious knowledge. If humans never had a thought that was different from the ones imposed by the regime that organises their society, then human evolution would not have happened and would stall right now. It is "the freedom" to have such a thought that fuels that growth process, that development. It is "the freedom" to think differently that allows science to move forward.

In order for humanity to grow, individuals need to have freedom of thought, speech and action. As we have seen before, this is also an absolute requirement for individual health. Now it turns out that an individual free will is a requirement for human evolution. And specifically, individual free will is needed to allow the societies that human beings construct to evolve in the direction life takes humanity. Nature takes humanity in the same direction, following the same rules, it takes the entire creation too.

This means that humanity is supposed to learn, to become conscious of, what nature is and what it already knows, always has known. Humanity is the process of bringing consciousness to the creation. Our consciousness is to develop towards understanding what life and nature is all about. That is also why free will does not affect the path of evolution human beings and the universe are on. It does, however, affect what humanity as a group expresses. A single life is easy and simple when we blindly follow orders, rules and instructions. Life itself, however, requires curiosity, investigation, and difference of opinion. This is in effect having the freedom of will, the freedom to believe something different. This is not a threat to natural evolution. This is a threat to any restriction imposed upon any free-thinking individual by others, and the free-thinking individual then becomes a threat to the group as free will is not compatible with an imposed way of life, a manufactured society.

The free will of an individual does not change the natural path of that individual.

The free will of an individual does change humanity.

The free will of an individual rips apart societies founded on illusionary beliefs about life.

The free will is a tool that allows life and the universe to become conscious of itself.

> *"Every form of control and suppression is a form of distortion and therefore violence."*
>
> **J. Krisnamurti**

COMMUNITIES AND SOCIETIES

The smallest group in the human species consists of a man and woman coming together and producing a child. This unit we call family. The family needs to work together to provide all the basic needs like food, shelter and security for them to survive and even thrive. When families come together we call this a community. The idea of living in a community is to share the work together in order to make life easier, and as we are social creatures, to make life more enjoyable and fun. This sharing we call *cooperation*.

I have seen these small communities in the Peruvian Amazon where we spent a year living in the big jungle city of Iquitos. When we had free time, we would get on a local river boat that goes along the river to and from Iquitos, stopping at all the small villages and communities along the way. It was very clear that the smaller the community, the simpler the life was. In small communities' life seemed to be totally driven and guided by nature. The seasonal river levels meant that fishing would be done in accordance with the river level. In a flood area houses would be built so they could float in high season, or on stilts, so they would stay above water levels. They all ate seasonal food so the time to sew and pick crops was dictated by nature too. This would give them times of heavy work and times of rest.

There seemed no need to organize things as nature and their own needs told them what needed doing. The best fishermen would fish, the best hunters would hunt, the best builders would build, and the right people would look after the food gardens and wild picking, and they all knew who to go to if someone came down ill. This all just happened naturally without committees, voting or organized political systems, at all. It just got done. If a man and woman joined together then the community would come together and they build a new house and have a celebration afterwards. The community seemed to have a balance of the right people and characters. If tensions were getting ready to get out of control, and a dispute could not be dealt with, then one of the families in the dispute would simply pack up and move further down river and start a new community rather than stay and go to war and possibly destroy the existing community. This peaceful solution is something that we in the "civilised" world could learn from these "simple" people. These people could live freely and the idea they were not free would be a strange concept to them.

The bigger the village and the closer to Iquitos, you could see more modern aspects of living. These villages had become heavily politicised and the people were "citizens", and being citizens had certain rights, obligations, and responsibilities. They were in the middle of two worlds, and it seemed the government was keen to nudge them further into their world. Here you would see the start of organisation and rules. The government would give money to the community to set up programmes like education or electricity and the community had to organise to put the money to use. Here you would now start to see an attitude of working as a community for the community, a change from working for yourself as an individual, but within a community.

We went to visit one village, a typical working village, as we wanted to avoid any tourist type Indian village just putting on a show. We got there and a young boy asked us to walk about a mile outside to visit a "native" community. We followed the boy through the jungle surrounding his village and came across a traditional looking roundhouse and people dressed in native dress. We were just out for a wander around a working village to soak up the reality of life in the Amazon, and maybe to have some local food, and we had not anticipated visiting this tribal community. We sat down and started talking and they offered to do a traditional dance for us which we said "thank you, but no", as we were really just out walking and passing by. They displayed their local crafts and we took a shine to the hand-crafted blow darts. We bought a couple and to our surprise they said the money was for the individual who made it and not the community. Maybe this wasn't a fully native tribe on the edge of civilization, but it was clear that the idea of things for the community was taken over by things for the individual.

Then you get people who have decided to go from the village to make a life for themselves in the city. The "bright lights theory" is when people get attracted by the lights of the big city, believing that the grass is not only just taller, but greener. Sadly, most of these people end up a lot poorer than they were in the village, and what they had there for free, they now had to work all hours of the day for. These people normally live in unsanitary slums, but the new life is hard to give up as the hope they may do better tomorrow is just in view, and so close they can almost touch it. In reality it may as well be a million miles away for most. A few will make it and get out of the slums and into the modern world with all it has to offer, but the vast majority get stuck in the hard life of the slums and it becomes the "new normal" and most stay and life goes on from there.

When you get to Iquitos, you see the need for mass organisation. So many people, approx. 450,000 living spread out over a large area, but more condensed in the centre, requires mass organisation. For example, roads need to be built and maintained, rubbish has to be collected, and dealt with, water and sewage are needed directly to the houses, hospitals, schools, markets, and all the rest that goes into building and maintaining a city and its population. The idea is that these rules that come out of the need to organise are made for the benefit of the people, and are created to make life easier for all. The reality is that it never turns out that way. Humanity is nowhere near mature enough to maintain a large society like this whilst at the same time maintaining freedom and quality of life. Corruption is inevitable and political ideologies take over from people who believe they know better. The political system has manifested.

Government = mind control
From Latin verb gubernare = control
From Latin noun mens = mind

You may say this is a coincidence and it's not what was meant, but it's clear that if you control the minds of the people, you control the people. Whether a coincidence or not, it seems a very accurate description as to what is happening.

Political systems

Democracy. Republic. Monarchy. Communism. Socialism Fascism Dictatorship Oligarchy Autocracy Technocracy

These are really just the main types of systems mankind has created. The thing to understand is that none of them equal freedom. Some openly have total disregard for individual freedom, whilst others gloss over it by making people believe the system is working for their benefit. Basically, you have a vote on who your dictator will be.

In the words of Aldous Huxley: "The perfect dictatorship would have the appearance of a democracy, but would basically be a prison without walls in which the prisoners would not even dream of escaping. It would essentially be a system of slavery where, through consumption and entertainment, the slaves would love their servitudes."

Now it becomes clear why all the warmongering elites of the so called "free" western world are going around the world invading and bombing countries in the name of "freedom and democracy". The trick here is to convince people freedom and democracy are the same thing and that having a vote is you expressing your freedom and confirming you live in a free society. Like some aware person said once, "If voting ever made a difference, they would make it illegal".

Just look at the political map of the world and the geographical map. One is a construction of the mind and one actually exists in the real world. Although the political map is a mind construct, it is not actually that far detached from nature.

Animals and even tribal humans make their own territories. They also mark them out and decide how they are going to live in their own space. They don't tend to have much interest in what is happening in other territories and issues only seem to arise at the borders of each territory. Violence is a last resort as the only goal seems to be to live in peace with neighbours as long as they don't invade your land. You live life your way, and I live mine my way, but don't cross into my life and impose yourself here. Thank you.

Human territories are called countries. Some countries may come together to make a bigger block of countries, like the EU. These countries are divided by imaginary borders with imaginary lines, mainly set on natural boundaries or human made fences or walls. But again, the idea is one set of people live in one place and decides the rules to which they want to live by, and another set of people in another place set their own rules so they too can live how they deem fit for themselves. All fair and well if people and countries are left to do as they wish and as they decide. Going around the world and bombing another country and their people as you do not like how they live in the name of "freedom and democracy" seems a strange way to promote peace in the world. If all the militaries in the world decided just to stay at home and defend their own countries it would be impossible for war to start. You do it your way, and I do it my way, but don't come over here imposing your will on me, sounds fair to me.

The idea that the leaders of the "free West" have some kind of moral obligation to go around the world killing people who don't have their values, and even using excuses like "weapons of mass destruction", has shown us the insanity of thinking we know better. It must be clear now that ALL wars are decided upon by men in closed meetings, who have their own agenda, and that in effect, *all* armies are really *corporate* armies working, whether knowingly or unknowingly, for the benefit of the men in suits whose only goal is to control governments, resources and people. The books, *Wall Street and the Rise of Hitler* and *Wall Street and the Bolshevik Revolution*, both by Antony Cyril Sutton, show how western bankers funded communism and fascism into power, while residing in, and funding, the democratic West. When you fund all sides, and all sides go to war, you always win and make a literal financial killing in the process. "War is a Racket", as Smedley D. Butler said.

It does not really matter what political system is in place, the real issue is who is behind it and what their intentions are. A dictatorship under Ghandi is surely a more inviting and just system than a democracy under Tony Blair. A monarchy, where the King or Queen serves the people, is a better one than one that rules over the people. Whatever system we choose to go along with, it has to be clear that the system should be there to serve the people and not the other way around.

DIVIDED AND CONQUERED

One tactic used by elites over the centuries to enslave people is "divide and conquer". Something the Spanish did very well in Latin America when massively outnumbered, and the British Empire became experts at when building the biggest empire the world has known. When you don't really have the physical power to enslave a group of people, then getting them to argue amongst themselves is the perfect way to fragment any possible resistance, and to get them to build their own prison, while you just sit back and control the mess these people have been manipulated into creating.

In modern times, what is known as "Cultural Marxism" is the name given to the technique used by our controllers to get the masses arguing again amongst themselves, and to build their own prison. Under Marxist understanding, it's all about the oppressor and the oppressed. It does seem there is an oppressive class in this world, and the vast majority of humanity is in the oppressed class, But Cultural Marxism is being used to get the oppressed seeing the other oppressed people as their oppressors. It's a total manipulation that means the masses cannot even begin to see where the real oppression is coming from. If people want to know where this manipulation is coming from, they need to research the WEF, the UN, the World Bank, billionaires like George Soros, and the insidious Common Purpose charity.

Here we will look at some of the ways we are being divided and conquered, and we will try and take a more mature look at these subjects to see if a solution is possible for people who are clearly different, to unite. It is important to have these debates as people's freedoms are being taken away in the name of freedom. Sounds a bit confusing, but this is the reality with the laws that are being passed today. We need a way to defuse the situation and we need to agree to disagree.

Black Lives Matter

Anthony Johnson 1600 – 1670

In 1620 a black Angolan, later to be known as Anthony Johnson, was captured and sold into the Atlantic Slave Trade. He was bought by a colonialist in Virginia and worked as an "indentured servant" on a tobacco farm.

After 1635 he had served his contract as a servant and became a legally free negro man. In 1647, with the purchase of a calf, he entered the legal record as a free man. He became a successful land owner, acquiring 250 acres by 1651 and he started his own tobacco farm with his own five indentured servants, four white and one black.

In 1653 John Casor, a black indentured servant to Johnson, claimed his indenture had expired years earlier with another owner and was therefore being illegally held by Johnson. Casor was offered work by a neighbour, Robert Parker, and signed a term of indenture with Parker. Johnson took this to court in

1654 and lost, but in 1665 in a Northampton court appeal the ruling was reversed and it was stated that Johnson still "owned" John Casor, and he was to be returned to Johnson.

This piece of history is put in here to make people think that the history we are given is never the whole story and clearly shows that the idea of only white people enslaving black people is not the whole truth to say the least.

Fast forward to 2013, and the creation of Black Lives Matter in the US. Allegedly a grass roots social movement, it got worldwide exposure in May 2020 with the murder of George Floyd by policeman Derek Chauvin. George Floyd was a convicted criminal with crimes including "aggravated robbery with a deadly weapon". The mentioning of him being a violent criminal is not meant in any way to excuse the horrific way he was held down by police. But let's go back to July 2011 to another case that very few people outside of California will know about.

In Fullerton, California, Kelly Thomas, a 37 year old homeless man with schizophrenia, was beaten to death by six members of the Fullerton Police Department. Medical records show that bones in his face were broken and he choked on his own blood. Police had been called to suspicious behaviour and Thomas was uncooperative and resisted when they attempted to search him. The video footage of the beating and tasing of a defenceless man is so horrific, there is no need to repeat the details here. The point is police brutality in the US seems to be non-discriminant, and thugs in uniforms will be happy to use their power over defenceless people, regardless of colour. There were no world-wide protests or movements for Kelly Thomas. I guess he was the wrong colour and no political gain could be made from his death.

What happened after the George Floyd death was promoted by politicians around the world, especially the western world; and in a time of national lockdowns for "the pandemic", these protests were allowed to go ahead almost unhindered. This was clearly a political agenda, or business as usual, for the manipulating elite. The fact that when people state, "*All Lives Matter*", they are shouted down for being racists tells you really what this movement, seemingly a mainly white middle class, middle-aged, movement in the UK, is all about.

Martin Luther King Jr, and his quote, "I have a dream that my four little children will one day live in a nation where they will not be judged by the colour of their skin, but by the content of their character", seems to be lost on these activists, who instead of trying to unite humanity, and moving forward from the divisions of the past, are actually trying to rip us apart again, and create a racist divide that is not really there.

White Privilege

Out of the same movement as BLM, we now get "white privilege". So let's take another quick look into history to get a better perspective. The history of the "Slave Triangle" is well known and well taught in schools, especially in Manchester, in Northern England. It is very clear there were three main parts to the triangle. A quick look at this triangle will show a slightly different story than the overwhelming one of only black slavery. This is not to play down the treatment of black people, and the enslavement of them, but to again just show it was part of a bigger picture.

Black people from Africa were taken over to the US to work on the cotton fields. They worked in the cotton fields as slaves. The cotton was then exported to Manchester and the surrounding area in Northern England to be processed in the cotton mills. So, let's be very clear, one third of the slave triangle were white men and women in Manchester tenements.

Another thing to look at is the activists' claim that all white people are inherently racist and have a privileged position in society because of their skin colour, and in turn they should feel guilt. So, let's break this down. I am a white male born in working class Manchester. Am I the oppressed or the oppressor here? Does family history of being working class in Manchester, and therefore part of the Slave Triangle, get overpowered by the fact that I am white? I am white but like many working-class Mancunians have Irish blood. The Irish, although said to be a different culture, are also deemed to be white, but they have a history of being oppressed too, by the English. So, are the white Irish oppressed or oppressors? What on earth does that make me? How much guilt should I have for being a white oppressor and how much anger for being part oppressed? Now things are going to get even more complicated! My wife is Peruvian, obviously oppressed. She is part native Peruvian and part black, so she is totally oppressed then. She is married to me, a man, part of the ruthless patriarchy. It couldn't really get any worse for her as 21 years of marriage and three kids seems to show!! Wait!! Our kids then are one quarter native Peruvian, one quarter black Peruvian, one quarter white English and one quarter white Irish. So how much guilt should they feel? They certainly look mainly white, and at one glance would surely be white racist, privileged and anything else you would throw at them. Yet their blood clearly shows they are more non-white than white. So, shall we judge them by the colour of their skin or by their true heritage? Should they now be at war with themselves? The parts Native Peruvian and Black at war with the White English side? Though not all because part of the white English was oppressed in the Slave Triangle. The Irish side is so confused it will have to just sit it out on the side-lines and have a beer.

And now we also have the possibility that a white man can identify as a black man, making us all so confused we all have no option but to go to the pub with the Irishman who identifies as an Irishman.

Yes, this is the absolute nonsense of the White Privilege argument. The truth is there is a privileged class in this world and they are not a particular race or nationality. Read the book, *The Open Veins of Latin America* by Eduardo Galeano, and you will see there is a privileged class and the international bankers and corporate elite at the World Economic Forum. May I add many religious organizations are where you need to start your search.

Teaching this, especially to young white children making them feel guilty over things they know nothing about, and have no connection to, is not only creating more division, but even more confusion, leading to more mental health problems and insane activism that is destructive and not constructive.

Again, we have a very simple solution here. If as a white person you have all this guilt over how racist and privileged you are, and your suppression of black people, then simply give all your wealth, including your house, business and money to any random black person without checking their background, and you will at last be able to rid yourself of your guilt and have a good night's sleep.

Yes, I've never seen so many guilty, privileged white people turn away and run out of sight. If you are going talk the talk, you must walk the walk.

Racism and the "cult" of culture

"The ideas, customs and social behaviour of a particular people or society"

Let us remember it is the incoming information from the environment that will trigger a response which in turn is what we call behaviour. All environments are different, some more than others. So on a diverse planet you would expect diverse people and therefore diverse cultures. With a community living close to nature, it will be the local environment, including the climate, local food and local resources, that will contribute massively to the local culture. For example, in the Amazon Basin the heat will dictate what clothes are worn and what housing is needed. The changing seasonal river level will dictate where to build a house, or as some do, to build a house on stilts or even houses that will float when the river level is high. This will also dictate when and where to go when out fishing and what type of fish you would expect to catch and how. Then local food may be seasonal, delivering different types of food. There may be certain times of the year for planting and certain times to pick the crops. All these things are dictated by the local environment and the people go with it and do what is needed whenever it is needed. This in turn creates what can be called cultural behaviour. Add to this humanity's love of music and dance, which means that after a period of hard work for a community there may be a time of rest and a time to celebrate the done task. With this free time a celebration of the task may manifest through music, dance, food, local wine and festivals. Maybe in a small community a new couple gets married and with no real organization the community come together and build a new home on a plot of land for the newlyweds. Again, a celebration of the new couple and the new home may become a custom and things then tend to get done in a certain way that suites the local community. All of this could be said to be natural culture that comes out of a balanced relationship with the local community and the local environment.

But when we look at the world today, and in the past, we see a lot of culture dominated by organized religion, superstition and manipulated trends. In modern times especially we see culture being manufactured by psychologists and public relations. People are creating beliefs and perceptions through the use of media, education, consumerism and government policies.

So instead of culture being a natural expression of a community and its relationship with the environment, which in turn maintains the connection to nature, and its guidance that promotes freedom of expression, we are now seeing even more than ever, with the use of modern technology, a fake culture, creating behaviour that is actually disconnecting us from nature and true knowledge, and creating cultural behaviour that is destructive to the individual and the community, and even cultural habits that are disturbing and violent.

At the same time the "multi-cultural agenda" is spreading from the West all over the globe. We are being told that culture is a great thing, should be embraced and welcomed. Maybe if the people of the world were coming together in the name of music, dance, food and celebration this could well be seen as a good thing. The problem is major parts of culture are religious beliefs, superstition and a lack of tolerance for others. Then we have male and female genital mutilation. One, male genital mutilation is accepted by some as a religious right; the other, female genital mutilation is said to be a crime. Now, as both are really the same thing, the mutilation of a child, why is one accepted by some and the other not? Surely ALL forms of mutilation on a child are clearly wrong regardless of beliefs or superstitions.

Then we have arranged marriages, oppression of women, oppression of homosexuals, forced religious worship, or worship of the state and more. There was a documentary many years ago that exposed one sub-Saharan country with a black population that had the horrific statistic of more young girls being raped than could read, with many of the rapes being carried out by the father or close family. Even just walking out in the street set them up to be raped by any man who wanted a power trip. We have the Rotherham Muslim rapist gangs who were raping white English young girls, but were ignored by the local police and council due to not wanting to be seen as being racist. This same thing has been happening in Sweden since the mass migration of Muslims into their country by the invitation of their own government. Again this has to be kept quiet and anyone complaining is deemed racist themselves when it's clear these Muslim gangs are specifically choosing white girls to commit their crimes.

There was also a documentary showing young girls in a northern Africa country with a culture of beating young girls to force feed them milk. Why? Because in their culture it was a sign of wealth if a man had a fat wife.

So, it's clear, not all culture is good. Therefore, multi-culture cannot be all good. I arranged a talk a year before the Brexit vote in the UK in Cornwall and I invited Brian Gerrish of the UK Column to speak regarding the multi-cultural agenda. I went around Penzance talking to people on the street, and shopkeepers, to ask their opinion and most people were scared to even have an opinion for fear of being called racist. For most people the reason they were against going into the EU was we already had enough of our own problems, like homelessness, and need for our own people, who are already here, than to open borders and welcome the whole of Europe. Also, many could see their own culture was dying and being threatened by multi-culture and many people still believe in the idea of a sovereign nation. A local man working in community politics actually said to me, while he was accusing me of being racist for no other reason than saying the international bankers are criminals, that he "wanted to see a multi-cultural Penzance". Just think about that for a moment. This man, a local small-time politician, was not happy with the local mainly white Cornish community, him being a local white man, so much so that he wanted to change it into a multi-cultural town. So my question was, is he racist against white Cornish people? This seems a fair question and proves that multiculturalism is a political agenda and not coming in a natural way from the people. In fact, when you ask, the vast majority of people, the indoctrinated youth an excepted, are actually against it and want to keep and protect their own culture. To be clear, this has nothing to do with skin colour or race. This is about culture, meaning how people see themselves, life, and how they wish to behave.

Not all culture is good. In fact, most cultural behaviour and customs seem to be the opposite of good. A person wanting to reject a foreign culture that they do not approve of is certainly not racist, and in fact, it is a normal defence system to make us aware of the unknown and part of our self-protection. "When in Rome …". If people want to move around the world freely in a natural and organic way, then that's fine, and they should be allowed to do that. They will find an area that suits them and will find their own tribe of like-minded people. In fact, this natural and organic flow of people stops a culture from stagnating and going bad. All life must flow, change and adapt, to survive, just like a river, and a community stagnating in its cultural outlook will become toxic like a stagnant pond, and eventually become self-destructive.

It seems the main issue behind racism is culture and not race at all. For example, a black man born in England, out of three or four generations of family here, will be basically culturally English. His behaviours, food taste and sense of humour will basically be typical of his local area. A black man who came over as a child from Africa or the West Indies would be a mix of the two cultures. An adult black man recently over from Africa will be a pure representation of the culture he came from. All these three hypothetical black men will be different and therefore seen to be different by the local English people, regardless of their colour. It could be quite possible all three black men have nothing in common and don't particularly even like each other. It would seem the local population would see these three men differently with the born and four generation bred black man being accepted as one of their own, and the newly arrived being looked at with caution, reservation and even fear. Mistrust of what you do not know is again a natural defence and does not mean someone is racist. A love of your own culture and wanting to protect that culture is not racist. Wanting to live with and work with people you know and understand is not racist.

In a hypothetical situation, what if a mother in Sweden had an emergency and needed someone to look after her thirteen year old daughter for a few hours at home. She has one neighbour who is a local white Scandinavian born and bred Swedish man and the other a Muslim immigrant man. Whom would she trust and choose to look after her thirteen year old daughter? Most people would be afraid to say for fear of being racist, but it would clearly be the local Swedish man. I'm pretty sure even all those wanting immigration and multi-culture in Sweden, when faced with that choice, would do the same. Why? The answer is simple, and it is part of our natural defence to make the best decisions we can in vulnerable circumstances. It is to do with observing the environment and says more about the culture of the new people rather than their skin colour.

The multi-cultural agenda is, in fact, the end of real local and national culture and a mishmash of all sorts of customs and beliefs, most of which are not valid or connected to the local environment. It may be great to see in some big cities, but for the general population it is the death of centuries' old cultures, and in fact, a mono-culture of fast-food eating, screen watching, celebrity worshipping people, detached completely from who they really are, but with a sprinkling of original cultural music and food to give the illusion it's still real. Anyone wanting to protect local culture, especially in European and British countries, is deemed as racist and against culture by people who seem to be totally racist against white people, or native people, and have a clear agenda to destroy long standing culture. More Orwellian double speak.

It is clear now in England that the most oppressed individual is the white, Christian, heterosexual male, who has a belief of the natural family unit of man–woman-child being the foundation of society. This very same man is actually seen by society as the main oppressor, and just having this personal belief, even if he does not wish to impose it on anyone else, is seen as offensive.

To finish off the nonsense of racism it is acknowledged we are all energy and the physical body manifests this in certain ways in relationship to the environment. Our bodies are just our physical vehicle to experience this reality. It's the equivalent or arguing about the colour of your red car being better than your neighbour's blue car, when in fact it's how the car drives that shows up its real qualities.

Transgender

This is another very controversial and divisive subject that seems to come out of nowhere. So let's break this down. These are some of the definitions I have found. It is interesting that on looking for definitions on gender it seems that nowadays it is deemed a totally socially constructed "thing" and not connected to biological sex.

Biological sex – The structural and functional characteristics of a person or organism that allow assignment as either male or female; sex is determined by chromosomes, hormones and external and internal genitalia (gonads).

Gender – The characteristics of women, men, girls and boys that are socially constructed. This includes norms, behaviours and roles associated with being a woman, man, girl or boy, as well as relationships with each other. As a social construct, gender varies from society to society and can change over time.

Intersex – Intersex is the term that a person may use when they have both male and female sex characteristics. These characteristics include genitalia, hormones, chromosomes, and reproductive organs.

This actually is an easy problem to solve. You have your biological sex and that cannot change. You can cut bits off or add bits on, take hormones or supress hormones. What you cannot do is change what you physically are regarding biological sex. Anyone claiming that you can is simply delusional. Now what can change is your own perception of yourself, and if you want to call that your gender, then fair enough. It is your choice how you feel and how you see and perceive yourself in this world. The only thing you cannot do is impose that perception on other people. I may consider myself tall, dark and handsome and highly intelligent (I'm actually none of those, though again that is a perception), but I have no right to impose my view of myself onto others. The same applies in that anyone can have any opinion of me they like, even if I don't like it, and express that opinion but they have no right to impose that opinion on me and force me to agree. If I am offended by another's view of me, then tough. It's called freedom of speech, and that's fine as long as we don't harass or abuse someone purposely with our opinions. Imposing your gender on people is no different as imposing an adjective about you on someone. They are both perceptions, personal to you and you alone.

If the point of the transgender movement is to allow a person to fully express themselves, which is their claim, then surely wanting to impose their view of themselves in this world on others is actually oppressive and goes completely against freedom of expression. The controversy in Canada over bill C-16, which Jordan Peterson infamously spoke out against, shows how close we are now to "compelled speech", which means the end of freedom of speech, and is in fact, pure Orwellian mind control. Bills like this will eventually lead to crimes of hate speech, discrimination, and actual harm being allegedly committed by people simply for not allowing another person to impose their will and belief on themselves and even worse having an opinion that is different and deemed not the right one and offensive. All in the name of freedom of speech and expression of course! Humans think via words, to control the words someone can use, or not use, is to control how they think and in turn how they behave. This is something very real and I have actually debated a transgender activist who said to me that simply disagreeing with their interpretation of biological sex and gender is actually "trans-phobic and a hate crime". This is a very dangerous mind-set and yet is only being put forward by a small minority of people, bullying their way into controlling the rest of society to the extent it's now fully integrated into the education system, and although the vast majority of people disagree with them, they are simply too afraid of being labelled transphobic or of being accused of a hate crime and the consequences that may go with that

Freedom of expression and speech has to be for all, or it's not freedom of expression, it's tyranny. And the fact that if you want to open yourself to imagination and total freedom of expression, then defining yourself as "this" or "that", actually restricts true freedom and puts you in a limited box of expression. If you truly want to expressive yourself in an unrestricted way, then just being, without defining, is what is needed. I have had many debates with transgender activists and what they do is switch between gender and biological sex, so it's never clear what is being discussed. We are at the point now where they do not, and cannot, even define what a woman is and this has spilled over into education and politics where everyone is either too ignorant or too afraid to define a woman. If you cannot even define what a woman is how can you claim you are a woman regardless of your physical biological sex?

This has serious consequences in society, where now, a refuge for women abused by men, can be infiltrated by a man defining himself as a woman. This turns the safe place into a dangerous and insecure environment, exactly what the women went there to escape. Also, in England we now have the Girl Guides allowing boys who identify as girls into their club, and even able to shower with young girls. Young children in education are now having gender celebration days as young as four and one school in England even banned using the words "mother" and "father".

If it is possible for a biological man to physically change into a biological woman, or vice versa, simply by changing their perception of themselves and behaviour, then we would be able to say biological sex is malleable, something the transgender activists tell me. This though has never been shown to be true. Yes, there is an almost unlimited number of ways you can perceive yourself. I'm lost as to the numbers of gender pronouns that are out there now, but none of that can change your biological sex. And again, the seemingly complex issue of intersex has nothing at all to do with the argument of transgender activists as they claim any one can identify as a woman, which is true. But they also state anyone can be a woman without actually defining what a woman is.

The WHO (World Health Organisation) states: "Gender is used to describe the characteristics of women and men that are socially constructed, while sex refers to those that are biologically determined. People are born female or male, but learn to be girls and boys who grow into women and men. This learned behaviour makes up gender identity and determines gender roles. The WHO gender policy 2002 defines the terms below."

Again, here the WHO differentiate male and man and female and woman. But if I was to say to a man who identified as a woman he was still a male I have honestly no idea what the reply could be. It also states there is no connection between biological sex and gender expression, meaning one's perception of oneself and behaviour. If you take for example a male lion and female lion, then clearly the biological sex and behaviour is different, and the biological sex of a male lion, and its physical qualities, determine behaviour. He will be the one who protects the pride and plays his very specific role in procreation due to his genitalia and physical size. The female, on the other hand, will bear and nurture the cubs and do most of the hunting due to her speed and agility. This shows biological sex and behaviour is connected, and at least in animals, the biological sex will determine and drive behaviour.

Human beings, though, have what we call self-awareness and imagination. This allows us to create and express ourselves in many more ways. To state though that gender is totally socially constructed does not seem right at all. Yes, there is a wide scale of human behaviour, both in male and female. Not all men are the same, just as not all women are. Many men have what we call feminine qualities and many women have masculine qualities. This great variation is what we call diversity but there are traits and differences for both male and female. For example, if someone breaks into the house in the middle of the night, then instinctively the man would get out of bed and go downstairs with the baseball bat to confront the danger. That instinct is not a social construction, but comes out of his biology.

It is a simple fact: women cannot compete with men on a physical level. You just have to look at sports. There is no woman alive who could even last ten seconds in a boxing ring with any heavyweight boxer, let alone with Mike Tyson. Serena Williams, perhaps the most powerful woman tennis player, would not even get in the top ten thousand of male tennis players who ever lived, and as for competing with Usain Bolt, in sprinting well that is a non-starter. It has been shown now that men identifying as women, who then go on to compete in women's sport, dominate. Men and woman are clearly physically different and those differences affect our behaviour. People have a right to perceive themselves as they wish, but a woman perceiving herself as a man, would never beat Usain Bolt in a race, no matter how hard she trained.

It has been shown in Scandinavian studies that when you open out society to be truly egalitarian, men overwhelmingly choose jobs working with things and woman jobs working with people. Yes, when you truly give people freedom of opportunity, they tend to revert to the role connected to their biological sex. This is not to say a woman could not, and should not, be allowed to train to be a "fireperson". Simply, it should all be based on equality of opportunity and not equality of outcome. To have the best fire service, we want the best people for the job, whether male or female, black or white, or whatever else. We do not want to try and force equal numbers in the belief it is somehow more just or better for society.

True freedom means freedom of opportunity, and to have an area of society functioning at its best for the people, then we want the people better equipped for that particular job, regardless of that person being a man or woman or perceiving themselves as man or woman. We simply want to best person for the job.

The transgender activists and other extreme feminists also claim that the history of women, who they refuse to define, is also a history of male, again, no definition, domination through a system of a hierarchy they call the patriarchy. There, of course, is some truth in this in many cultures, but, to be clear, the idea of a hierarchy is that it is built on ability and competence for the task in front of us.

If I have an idea that I wish to manifest into a reality and that idea, say building a school, requires more than one person then straight away I have created the need for a hierarchy. I may put myself at the top of the hierarchy, me being the one with the idea, and then the hierarchy is built on who is needed to do each particular job. Maybe an architect and an engineer will be the next level, then all the different trades needed for the project will make up the layers. Maybe the cleaner will be at the bottom of the hierarchy as you would not want a cleaner to be in control of building a safe structure housing children. This is in no way meant as a put down to the cleaner. It is simply how we organize to create. ALL people in the hierarchy are important and have their role to play and this is not about dominance, but about competence and having the abilities for the particular role in the project. Yes, a hierarchy can be built on dominance and that tends to be a male quality, but the idea that hierarchies are purely about male dominance and the tyrannical patriarchy is not a true and full picture of history, and of the present day, of how things actually work. In fact, if you look at society, and especially political leaders of today, it seems the women at the top are just as tyrannical as the men. In fact, I would say now that the whole political system is a hierarchy of tyranny in which men and women seem to be, at last, equal in that they are both as tyrannical as each other.

The general role of men is to provide and protect, and the woman to nurture and to be the homemaker. As we are highly evolved beings, and are able to use unlimited imagination, and due to the fact we are an evolving species nowhere near having reached its potential, then we are at a stage where we are breaking free from past restraints on our expression of life. This could lead to a change in roles and I have seen certain situations where the woman had a really good income before starting a family, and the man unable to work, so the man basically became the homemaker and the woman the provider. This would mean the man getting in touch with his nurturing side which he has and manifesting that more and I have seen this work. But let's be clear, it does not make him less of a man, and her less of a woman, as when in the middle of the night the window gets smashed it will still be the biological man jumping up and going down stairs with the baseball bat.

The only solution to this divisive issue is for everyone to be allowed to go their own way. We can all have our opinions and that is fine, but we must be able to agree to disagree, so that we can all be allowed to express ourselves freely and pursue knowledge and happiness on our own terms through our own chosen experience. Let us leave the judgment to nature itself and allow everyone to be responsible for their own actions and whatever consequences those actions bring. Certainly, let's not blame other people, when through our own decision making, our life starts to get difficult and starts to hurt.

Real tolerance means allowing everyone to express themselves as they wish as long as they don't impose it on anyone else, regardless of our own personal opinion. Real acceptance is just letting other people be, knowing they are on their own personal life journey.

There is one thing that I feel is totally wrong about this new out-of-nowhere ideology being pushed onto children as young as four in the education system. These beautiful unique little human beings, who are still trying to find their way and understand and discover who they are, are being given one powerful and damaging message: "You may be defective". What a start to life! Instead of embracing this little new life for what it is, the perfection of what it is, and let it develop in its own way, we have already put a message in its system that there may be something wrong. This is the real issue here and I feel the mental health consequences of this message will be hard to undo. But it is those who choose to take this path with their own families who will have to own the outcome and take responsibilities for it.

In the end, nature pursues balance and is the ultimate judge, not you and I. To judge that nature has made a mistake in creating a new baby boy when it maybe should have been a girl is ignorance and arrogance beyond belief. If nature has seen it fit for a life to exist the way it is, then I think a better path to take would be to embrace all life and diversity, as it is, and not try to create what is not.

Intersectionality

"The interconnected nature of social categorisations such as race, class, and gender as they apply to a given individual or group, regarded as creating overlapping and interdependent systems of discrimination or disadvantage."

The previous subchapters are some examples of how human beings are being actively encouraged to be divided and conquered. Being divided makes it a lot easier to be controlled by the people who wish to control us.

To sum it all up, intersectionality is the name given to how the individual is divided into many parts. Parts that according to the "experts" are either oppressor or oppressed. There does not seem to be any concept here of just being. To some extent we are all oppressors or oppressed and that is something "they" deem has to be rectified. Again, this is why this whole movement has been given the name "Cultural Marxism" because it makes clear divisions between the two categories. This creates an attitude of you are my friend or my enemy, or you are with me or against me. And to repeat, this is all done in the name of freedom of expression, ah, but only if you agree.

The only way out of this is to just not get involved and let everyone just be and follow their own path. Debating with people who are controlled by an ideology is futile. It is good to understand these people and have your own clear opinion for when it is needed, but really, if you can, it's just best to walk away and wish them well. Most of the people promoting this divisive ideology actually believe themselves to be spiritual people who have been oppressed and held back by society, and are completely unable to grasp the idea of true freedom and self-responsibility.

True freedom means accepting things you like and things you don't like, and having the choice to partake or not, and certainly not imposing your version of freedom on others. True freedom means freeing yourself from restraints of perception and breaking out of the box, not bringing in more tags, names, and boxes to close down perception and therefore expression even more.

Veganism

Another subject that seems to cause so much friction and even hatred amongst people is what food we should be eating. The vegans state we are naturally herbivores, mainly because that without man-made tools, we could not hunt and kill, and because of our connection to the apes.

So, first of all, chimpanzees eat meat, even their own kind, so that kind of clears that up. Next are the teeth and tools. Well let's remember mankind is an evolving species and evolution means change. Our more open consciousness and imagination has allowed us to develop tools to hunt and live in places we could not live in before. The Inuit being a classic example.

This shows that our digestive tract is easily able to adapt to a change in food, and the Inuit seem to be able to survive in a wilderness which would have been impossible before tools had come our way.

The main issue it seems, though, is emotional. The phrase "meat is murder" is widely used to convince people, through an emotional argument, that killing an animal to eat is the same as murder. We can understand completely why individuals would see it this way and I'm sure most of us have thought deeply about this too. Life and death, hunter and prey, are all part of the glory of nature. The lion eats the buffalo, the tiger the deer, the snake the rat, and so on. There is a clear relationship here that in the animal kingdom is not judged; it just is. To say we are not part of that is to say we are not part of nature itself.

Yes, we are evolving, and our new awareness, and the coming to the fore of our emotional aspect, is causing us a great deal of confusion, and now we have started to judge. We are, though, judging nature itself, something that we have very little understanding of, even though we are part of it. We can see why many people have problems with this, and it is actually possible that we could evolve not to eat meat due to this emotional connection we have to other animals. It may even be possible that in the very far future we will evolve to not need physical food at all, and are be able to get all the energy and information we need purely from an energetic source, which is unlimited and all around us. But for the time being, we are where we are, collectively and individually.

The main issue here is the treatment of our animal companions on this planet. The Alpaca herders of the Andes and reindeer herders of Scandinavia, have a very close and caring relationship that suits both human and animal, and yet they regularly kill an animal for food, clothing and tools. Leafcutter ants are an example of farming in nature. The relationship they have with the leaves they bring into their home to farm the fungus which they eat, makes them basically mushroom farmers. The herder ants herd aphids for the surgery food they produce after feeding on plant life. It is said the ant produces a chemical on its feet that tranquilise the aphids to keep them close by therefore controlling them. Relationships like this are everywhere in nature. So even farming animals is a natural process. We are all for animal welfare, and some struggle with the idea of killing to eat, but we also need to realise that it is part of nature and it would be wise for us not to judge something we do not fully understand.

In the end, the solution is the same, you live as you see fit, and allow me to do the same. All happy. It is also worth knowing that the vegan agenda is being heavily pushed by the global elite and not just for health or animal welfare, but "to save the planet" as we shall now see.

Saving the planet

This, like many issues, is an enormous subject we could spend all-day cherry-picking data trying to prove a point, or an ideology. First to accept is that change is the universal constant. Without change there can be no life because life itself is movement, and movement means change. There are clear recorded times in the history of this planet when the climate has been just about everything it can be. It seems a lot of this comes and goes in cycles, cycles of thousands of years and even shorter ones like "El Niño" of just a few years.

Scientists have discovered that roughly every 20,000 years, the Earth shifts its axis, meaning that over the last 240,000 years, the Sahara has gone through multiple periods of wet and dry climates. The last "green" period ended around 5,000 years ago and led to the growing desertification of the region.

So there is nothing static in regard to the earth's climate. In fact, it's quite the opposite. The argument that fossil fuels have increased the temperature of the earth, and are now pushing us to disaster, is pure speculation. In fact, many scientists have shown it's temperature that pushes up carbon in the atmosphere and not the other way around as we are led to believe. "Global warming" was quickly changed to "climate change" when it became clear we possibly just had a quick warm spell and things were not so bad after all. Saying that, many people were quite looking forward to that Mediterranean climate here in England. It would have certainly saved us money wanting to go to Spain for holidays. So we may have possibly had a hot spell, mass propaganda pushed out in the media and government agencies, of the emergency in front of us. We need to act now!! If we do not act now its curtains for all of us!! Wasn't that same propaganda used recently to put us into lockdown? The whole show, though, was emotional manipulation. Many of us can remember how all the polar bears were soon to be gone. One of the most majestic creatures on the planet was going to be wiped out and it's all our fault.

Let's see then how that worked out.

It was stated that in 1970 there were only about 5,000 polar bears left. The latest figure from 2020 shows at least 26,000, with even 31,000 or more being closer to the truth. Before the 1970's, hunting was a large part of the decline in population, but when that was stopped the populations grew back quickly. Yet despite a growing population we are still being told their numbers are in decline, but it's a decline that just hasn't happened. The experts now claim one third will be lost by 2050 due to climate change. They again put out figures of a population in decline, but it is just one individual population, in one area, due to many circumstances declining, and completely ignoring the fact that, overall, they are growing in numbers. But we are told to trust these experts as they know best. Zero of what they have predicted has come true, but it's a future truth and we'll just have to go along with it. The whole Global Warming and now Climate Change science was all put forward through scientific models predicting a future, and not based on what was actually happening.

In October and November 2019 photos of various cathedrals in the UK were pushed out through local and national media of the water levels almost as high as the spires at the top of the great buildings. Though the vast majority of people accepted this as a total exaggeration, the psychological impact still affects the vast majority by playing on their fears and emotions. Yes, the science of man-made climate change via CO_2 is purely a psychological one and has nothing at all to do with what is actually happening, or not happening. These were the same scientific models used to tell us we were all going to die if we did not lock ourselves in our homes, wear masks, disinfect our hands, keep away from other humans, and take experimental drugs and therapies.

As you can see in the book, *Medical Fascism* by Robert Ryder, what we were told and what actually happened was not the same thing. Again the whole show orchestrated by psychologists and "experts", manipulating us to perceive the world as they want us to perceive it and not as it actually is. If we want to look at climate in a scientific manner, we have to look at *all* the factors that may be present and not just one issue of artificially pumping what is commonly known as the "gas of life" (carbon dioxide) into the atmosphere. I think that big yellow thing in the sky should be taken into account first. Then we have the incredibly complex natural cycles, and if we want to look at mankind's influence, then I think we should include that chemical soup, many have called "chemtrails", coming out of planes that leave a criss-cross of something floating around. Contrails do not do that. Then again, we need to ask what is HARP? What are these installations and what are they being used for? The position of the earth's axis, the sea currents, air currents, and much more, are all things that can affect the climate.

I have seen the devastation of deforestation in the Amazon. And again, how much do isolated incidents speak for the whole of the Amazon? The toxic waste and rubbish dumped into its rivers every day are the real issues the Amazon is facing and these problems have been forced on people by big corporations and governments who now pass the buck and say it's the consumer's fault.

A big part of this problem is the money system and how that intertwines with the big corporations, and we will come to this later, but for most people who live day to day just to survive, the idea of sacrificing more to "save the planet", when they get up every day not knowing if they can feed their family, is totally irrelevant. The planet will be ok. It certainly will not be killed off by CO_2, and despite all the man-made chemicals we push into it, the planet has the ability to self-heal as all life does. If you want to become a voice for the planet, then look into the toxic rubbish being created and dumped freely, and without consequence, by the elite corporations. Look into the system that creates and permits that insanity and stop blaming the gas of life for a demise that is not coming. The whole vegan and climate change ideology has now become an anti-human ideology and the solution for many is to massively reduce the population for the sake of the planet. Only those pushing this agenda, the elite and the activists, consider themselves to be part of a humanity that must stay and it's the rest of us that are for the knackers yard. The planet is not overpopulated, it's just mismanaged. If the leaders really wanted to stabilise the population, then economic freedom and prosperity is the proven solution but that is clearly not on their agenda. The whole man-made climate change agenda is political and not scientific.

One final point on the issue is the manipulation of the insecurity of human beings. We are so detached from real life and nature that we have forgotten that nature has its own flow and that nothing is fixed. It has got to the point now where we feel threatened by nature itself, yes, that very same nature we are a part of. When people are lost or under threat, fear can easily take over and it is clear now mankind is totally lost psychologically and that fear is being manipulated to instil in us the need to control something that cannot be controlled and does not need to be controlled.

There have always been hot and cold periods on this planet and there probably always will be. It is up to us to adjust to the changing environment and go with nature, which humanity has the imagination and flexibility to do so if it just let go of trying to control. This need to control can actually be seen in many areas of life, in relationships, with finances, work, and more, and does not allow for freedom of expression and growth. It's all based on fear and not being able to live in the now. The world political system of control now is so totally out of control, or to put it another way, totally controlled, that we have no option but to just let go of planning the future, let go of our fears, and just live and respond to the ever changing now which is our natural state. If that is not a homeopathic message, I don't know what is. The planet is doing ok, its humanity that may not survive.

DIVIDED WE STAND
– UNITED WE FALL

Mankind is being pushed to live together under a set of rules that will totally constrict human expression. The tolerance and freedom of expression that claims to bring people together is actually dividing us even more. We are being told we have to tolerate anything the system says, and freedom of expression is for those people approved by the system. If you want to live a life outside of the systems boundaries, then that cannot be tolerated, and that freedom of expression is simply not allowed.

It is now very clear that people with very different perceptions of life, and who want to live very different lifestyles, cannot live in peace together. This forced peace, by suppressing anyone who has a different view from the accepted one, is like a ticking time bomb. As we know in illness, suppressing symptoms, and not allowing the body to do what it naturally wants to do, builds up toxicity in the system. It is no different in the mind when you suppress and do not allow an individual, or groups of individuals, to live a life and pursue happiness as they themselves deem fit.

The communitarian agenda to bring humanity together under one banner controlled by a One World Government can only lead to mass oppression, and as history tells us, even genocide. It's time to accept we are all different and want and need different things in our pursuit of happiness. We need to come together with other people who have our same vision and not the vision of the One World Government. We need to find our own tribe and allow others to do the same and not judge. Like the tribes in the Amazon, if we find friction is causing too much trouble we need to walk away and not try to sort out problems that cannot be sorted out, and we need to understand that that is ok too. We don't all have to be friends, but likewise we do not have to be enemies. You go your way, and I go mine, and we wish each other luck. Only by having this mature outlook on life will humanity be able to live in peace. If not, the future does not look good at all.

Money and Debt Slavery

If there is one thing along with imaginary rules and authority that control our lives it has to be money. On the surface it seems like an enormous subject requiring massive research as it seems even the most intelligent economics "experts" seem confused and not sure how to go forward.

As with most things in life that seem confusing, you have to go back to basics and ask:

What is it?

Where does it come from?

How does it function?

Here we will try to put forward the simple facts about money that will explain how and why the entire world seems to be bankrupt. As we are not trading with other planets, then it seems clear that the problems, and therefore solutions, come from the system in place on this planet.

What is money?

Money is, or at least should be, a representation of our productive energies to be passed around to get around the problem of bartering. We may want something someone produces or a service they offer, but we haven't got anything they want to exchange in return. So this little piece of paper (or now number on a computer) is exchanged, representing a certain agreed value, or amount of my productive energies, that can be redeemed at any time by anyone. So money being passed around is productive energies being passed around. The more you have of it would fairly represent your productive output. The more money in circulation would indicate lots of productivity and less money, less productive activity.

Just to be clear, everything we need in order to thrive has been given to us free by the Creator. The sun doesn't charge us to come up every morning, and all the resources we need and use are provided free by the planet. Money is not a necessity to create wealth, but just a tool to facilitate the fair passing of production. A fully conscious, compassionate, mankind could get on fine without it, but that doesn't mean there is anything wrong with a monetary system, providing it is being used fairly.

Where does it come from?

What we call cash is produced by the Central Bank via permission of the treasury. Through the Central Bank, the cash, real money, is passed into society when banks purchase notes and coins from the Central Banks to facilitate their banking with their customers - you. Here we are talking about normal day to day banking and not investment banking. In the UK, for example, this cash makes up approximately 3% of "money" in circulation.

The cash, coins and notes, produced by the Bank of England is debt free, and actually makes a profit for the Bank of England as the cost of producing the cash is pennies but it is sold at full value to the banks. After taking out costs, the Bank of England is able to pass on the profit to the treasury. So this means that about 97% of "money" in circulation is non-cash, what we now see as numbers on a computer screen. This new money is created as credit when people wish to buy a house, mortgage, or purchase an item without having the cash to do so, but intend to pay in the future.

Their agreement to pay in the future is what actually brings this new money into existence, what we call credit. The banks do not pass real money from one account to another to lend this money. They simply create it out of thin air and credit your account with the sum required. They will charge you for this service with what we call interest. So, for example, if you borrow £100,000 you may be expected to pay back £110,000 in total as £10,000 may be added in interest. The important thing to understand is the principle, amount of credit, is created. but not the interest.

Real money exists and circulates through society and only ceases to exist when it is taken out via taxes by the central government. Credit is taken out of circulation as it is paid off. This means the amount of money in circulation is lowered when people pay off their debts.

How does it function?

Central Banks are basically the "court Jews" of modern times. In the past usury, interest on loans, was universally condemned in the Christian world. In modern times, Central Banks have taken on this role. They have the role of facilitating loans on behalf of the government, controlling interest rates, keeping inflation below 2%, and they are the Banks of the Banks, and of the government. The issue of whether they are Private Banks or owned by the Treasury is irrelevant. The Bank of England came into existence as a Private Central Bank, but was Nationalised in 1946. The important thing to know is that its role never changed.

The main thing to understand is that most "money" comes into circulation as credit when people take out loans and mortgages. Only the principle is created and not the interest. Hence, the interest does not actually exist, which means that there is not enough money in circulation to pay off the debt. When this happens you basically have two options. Pay off the debt with something of real value like your car or house, or ask for more credit/debt to be created so you can keep up your debt payments. This system means that the only way people can pay off their loans is for others to keep creating more money through credit, thereby expanding the available money, but also expanding the debt. In turn, the ratio of debt top money available expands and we end up with a bankrupt nation.

As governments also borrow money this way, then this explains why the world is bankrupt to the money creating entities. When an individual is bankrupt, the banks come for the real wealth as payment. Your car, house, or business is repossessed. When a government is bankrupt then they have to sell off wealth in the form of privatisation of the real wealth like resources, energy and infrastructure. This also has a limit because in the meantime the debt is still growing. For example, the UK pays over £1 billion a week in interest payments alone on the government debt. Now imagine all the money in interest being paid to banks via mortgages, loans, and business loans. All this money gets filtered into the hands of very few people and we become slaves to debt, a debt created out of thin air.

When you see now that the Central Bank, and the banks themselves, control how much money is in circulation, and the Central Bank controls the interest rate, then it is easy to see why "boom and bust" exist. The Central Bank can keep interest rates low, which entices people into cheap loans and mortgages. Then when everybody is in debt, they can ramp up the interest rates, making people unable to keep up with the payments and having to sell their homes, cars, etc., to pay back what they owe.

Historically counterfeit money has been used as a weapon to bring down governments by making their money worthless. When we allow the Banks to control the amount of money in circulation, we are basically allowing them to control the country. Let's be clear, banks work for profit and not for people. The amount of money should be a representation of the productivity. When banks push billions into circulation, and at the same time the economy, the real economy is shut down, and the only outcome will be hyperinflation.

In 2008, the UK Government, like other governments, bailed out the banks via quantitative easing (money printing). This money went to the banks, who, instead of putting it into the real economy, horded it, invested it, and paid themselves massive bonuses for doing so. In 2020 the UK Government, like most other governments, actually shut down the real economy, and again brought billions of money into existence that went mainly to big pharma and medical products, medical technologies like "track and trace", and as most small independent business were forced to close, billions went to big businesses like Amazon, where many products are made through cheap labour in China.

The day to day banking we do is completely interconnected to the investment banking we call the global casino. This means what happens in one will affect the other, as in 2008. The gambling of investment banking can personally affect me and you, who may have no wish to risk our hard-earned money, and we will all go down together. None of this is an accident, and although the vast majority of economists are totally clueless about money, just as most doctors have no idea what the human body is and what disease is.

There are a few people at the top of the pyramid that know exactly how this works. If you keep this model of money and debt creation up for enough time, you will bankrupt the world and everyone in it, and when this happens there is only one option, and that is to pay back the debt with the real wealth which in reality is what they wanted all along. The end product is a world owned and controlled by a corporate elite and fully backed by the politicians claiming to look after us. This is worldwide treason.

The truth is, slavery was never abolished; it was rebranded. Debt slavery working with "free-trade" allows rich individuals to simply go around the world buying up and creating businesses which over time just filter all the wealth, the real wealth, into the hands of a handful of people, whilst the majority of mankind scramble around for the scraps.

When we add on to this the idea of "ownership" and the "person", we can easily show how a small group of individuals can take over the world. In Nature, animals and tribal people claim a land area. The concept of owning it is not real to them. If one animal or tribe want to take over the land of another, they will have to go to war for it. This, it seems, is far too much trouble for the Global Elite. They created the concept of "ownership" and that things can be bought and sold with money. So if something can be bought with money, and you have control over all of the money, then why not the possibility of everything becoming owned so you can, over time, buy up the whole world and everything and everyone in it. Yes, that includes you.

When you buy something, even then you are not really the owner, but the "registered keeper". This applies to land, a car, a house, or even your children. The real owner is "The System" itself and the people who run it. This is why governments can take children away from parents when they decide the parents are not bringing them up to the government's own standards. This is why the government can deem it necessary, at any time, to demolish your house if they decide it's an emergency. This is why in the UK, and many other western countries, people need permission to live on their own land, even if they are producing their own solar energy, have their own water and have a composting toilet. You are not truly the owner, but just an individual with permission under specific rules, allowed to, or not, to live on a piece of land.

The Rothschild family own 100% of The Wildlife Trust in the UK. Bill Gates is the biggest farmland owner in the US. Many other rich people own massive tracts of land throughout the western world and combined with corporate free-trade, the rest of the world is being bought up and controlled, which in turn creates dependency on the system for people who are not now even allowed to just live a self-sufficient life on the land in peace.

The system they use is one of words and Laws. They actually speak a different language to us called Legalize. The Law of the Land applies to human beings and is meant to stop people causing harm or loss to another. The mass of rules and regulations they use to control us come out of Maritime Law which is Corporate Law. It's all a form of mind-control.

This massive subject is well explained by the late John Harris on Youtube under "It's an Illusion": www.youtube.com/watch?v=NKvacmyLG2A

The thing to understand is that this whole show is an illusion built on myths.

- Money is fake wealth

- The system is built on fake laws

- Ownership is a fake construct

- The citizen is a fake being

When the illusion is revealed, it loses its power like the weak old man behind the curtain in the Wizard of Oz.

A just monetary system for all

So if we go back to money just being a representation of productivity, founded on creative ideas and natural resources, then here is my model for a fair and just system.

Stop government borrowing *now*. Government should not be allowed, and do not need, to borrow money when they can create it, debt free, themselves. Remember the government borrows more in YOUR name. In any other context that would be fraud.

Bring in complete Glass Steagall, complete separation of investment and commercial banking. This will also allow us to stop bailing out banks. No more bailouts. Let them fail.

Direct from the treasury we can produce our own credit, based on what we need to produce as a nation. Fiscal expenses that can go on roads, infrastructure, transport, and energy.

Nationalise the basic things of life to maintain society, such as utilities, water and energy, roads, main transport routes.

Ban all interest on loans. Introduce an upfront regulated service charge as a fee for extending credit. Then only the amount credited is to be paid back. This means the service charge will come out of the present existing money supply, so when the new money/credit is being created there will always be enough money in circulation to pay back the loan.

The money that is created by the treasury is interest-free and the only debt attached to it will be used in the building of roads, the supplying of energy and other things the money was produced for in the first place. The debt will be in making excellent use of the credit given, so it's a debt of creating more, like more jobs, and more wealth. Basically, anything we can imagine. We can produce the money needed to manifest it. This would be a great time to invest in real science and engineering, and a great time to pursue free energy.

Just as it is not good when the banking system has almost total control of the money supply, it would equally not be a good idea to let the government have all the control. Always spread the power out. A well-regulated system, where the banks can create credit for private businesses and people, where the borrower and lender are held responsible for the new money being productive, can work well.

We don't want to go into a communist style of money system with total government control. This is the failing of the Cuban Revolution. Yes, they kicked out the banks and international corporations, but they also took over everything, and took away the peoples' right to lead their own lives and to run their own businesses. We need motivation, inspiration, and incentive to work hard, and create and manifest our ideas, and the pursuit of material gain is not wrong in itself. Freely available interest free credit allows us to imagine and manifest our ideas and pursue personal economic freedom, not depending on big government to provide all our needs.

A debt free, interest free money system would mean we do not have to turn out rubbish and get it into landfill as quick as possible so the next batch of rubbish can be made and sold to keep up debt payments. This would be real sustainability and a real way to look after the environment as we could produce quality products that last and people can, if they wish, spend more time pursuing happiness than paying off debt.

Taxation can be used to control the amount of money in circulation so that it is in relation to production. Taking money out of circulation when productivity is low helps to prevent inflation and enables a steady balanced economy. Taxation gain can then be re-invested into new production and any shortfall for big projects can just be created again, instead of borrowing again. The amount of money in circulation should always represent the amount of productive activity.

At the moment there is plenty of work to be done, but in the present system, they say there's not enough money to fund it. Well, for God's sake, create it! Interest free credit, backed by the ideas we want to manifest. The resources we have, and the desire to work, means any idea or productivity can be made into reality, simply by producing the money to facilitate it. The needed work dictates the money supply and not the other way round.

This system will mean an end to international banking as we know it and the creation of masses of local community banks serving the community. This way money will no longer be seen as wealth in itself, but as it should be, a representation of our productivity. The people then controlling money creation will be dictated to by our production and not the other way around. With the end of huge international banks, and with the central government only responsible for national infrastructure, this would mean the end of wars as there would be no money to fund them. And with this model spreading worldwide, every country would have the chance to gain wealth for their citizens, so the need to compete would not be there. To manifest this throughout the world seems an impossible project. The truth is, if the City of London were to fall, meaning the Corporation of London, that would be the first huge domino that would set off an unstoppable chain reaction right around the world and the end of debt slavery as we know it. I would also add that maybe half of the world's problems, nationally and individually, would disappear overnight. Now that would make a very special day.

In the meantime, there is a more fundamental thing that needs to change, and that is our attitude and mind-set to money, value, and wealth. The world, whether we like it or not, is being deliberately pushed into financial and economic Armageddon. This collapse is being engineered by people at the WEF, who already have the solution, global socialism and dependency on governments, a One World Government. We cannot escape the collapse that is to come. It has to come, but how we get through it, and what lies beyond it is our choice. To get through it, we need an attitude of unconditional giving. This does not mean simply giving everything you have to all that ask, but giving to people in your community without the want of something in return. No amount of bartering or other ways around the system, like bitcoin, can get us through what is to come. Bitcoin they tell us is an uncontrolled decentralised token, but what is the worth of a token if you have nothing to trade. This shows us clearly now what real wealth is. You can have all the money in the world, physical or digital, but if you have nothing to trade or to give you have nothing at all.

An attitude of giving, just like the earth gives to us, will help us survive. And then when the time comes to choose where to go after the collapse, it seems wise not to go for the solution put forward by the same people who have created the problem. The WEF's Great Reset means total control and total dependency, a global technocracy where your every move, and even thought, is monitored. The way out starts with the mind-set of going your own way.

There was a man 2000 years ago who showed us an example of unconditional giving, but also showed us how to deal with these money changers. "And Jesus went into the temple of God, and cast out all them that sold and bought in the temple, and overthrew the tables of the money changers, and the seats of them that sold doves, And said unto them, It is written, My house shall be called the house of prayer; but ye have made it a den of thieves."

It's time to turn over the tables of the Banking Mafia.

GLOBAL LEADERS WITH
A COMMON PURPOSE

When conversing with people about the world situation they can see, when you take the time to explain, that the whole western world, at least, is being run in the same manner, with the same rules, the same pressures, the same beliefs, and the same political control. And yet, they totally reject the idea it is planned and organised as it is beyond what their belief and their imagination allows. They can see it, but at the same time they reject it because they can't see how it could be done.

The entire democratic West is basically run the same way. Yes, there are differences. For example, in the Commonwealth, we have common law made by the people, at least in theory, but on the whole, the system runs the same way. In fact, this system runs throughout the whole world as countries will have a department of health, education, finances, and transport, etc. This creates a pyramid structure in society where the policies for each individual sector are made by central government. In theory, especially in English common law countries, and especially the US, power starts with the local community and it is they who decide how their community is run, and which laws to be passed. The central government should not interfere with local policies. This system, though, has been infiltrated by "leaders" whereby central government policies, in fact UN policies, are being put in place at a local level.

The charity "Common Purpose" was exposed by former Royal Navy officer Brian Gerrish when he came across their influence in his local city of Plymouth, and then found it to be widespread through the country and beyond. This is taken from his website www.cpexposed.com.

"Common Purpose (CP) is a Charity, based in Great Britain, which creates *future leaders of society*. CP selects individuals and 'trains' them to learn how society works, who 'pulls the levers of power' and how *CP graduates* can use this knowledge to lead Outside Authority."

When I first came across Brian's work in 2010 it was the missing piece that showed me exactly how world governance was going to come about, and I named it "communism by stealth". It is actually very easy to achieve.

First you create departments that have authority over the people in certain areas as stated above. You then make sure as many people as possible, at the top of each department, think as you wish them to think, and share your same "vision" for the future. These *leadership programmes* are happening all over the world under the guise of encouraging local community power, but in fact are all pushing the same ideology coming straight out of the UN. Man-made climate change, gender pronouns, sex education, multi-culture, children's and women's rights, and now health security, are just some examples of UN policies being taken on by local regions and local communities, but in the belief they are making the decisions themselves, and that they are in control. There is clear evidence of NLP (neuro-linguistic programming) being used in these leadership programmes to get candidates to think in a certain way and see the world and humanity in a certain way, a way that furthers the agenda of the controlling elite. NLP could easily be said to be a form of hypnosis.

It is well known now that many western leaders have gone through the World Economic Forum's leadership training programme, including Boris Johnson, Emmanuel Macron, and Justin Trudeau. It is also known now, as founder Klaus Schwab stated, that Vladimir Putin has also gone through this programme. The world is clearly not what it seems to be. Who are the WEF and what are its goals? Here, direct from its website.

- "The World Economic Forum is the International Organization for Public-Private Cooperation."

- "The Forum engages the foremost political, business, cultural and other leaders of society to shape global, regional and industry agendas."

So we have unelected elites who serve their "stakeholders", clearly stating they have a mission through their "leaders of society" to "shape" the world and humanity.

This again comes down to the idea of an exterior expert who knows better than you do and knows what is best for you. These people clearly believe they know better than us, and though we are allowed our opinion, it is they who will make all the decisions in our life. Julia Midddleton, founder of Common Purpose, actually published a book telling us of the intentions of these trained leaders ("Beyond Authority: Leadership in a Changing World"). On the Common Purpose website, they now boast of having 105,000 leaders worldwide, 7,000 more participants each year, and are managing 100 large cities globally. Most people believe they vote for public servants and it is these elected politicians who are pushing local, national, and international policy, and who have real power and authority. The truth is that these elected politicians are just a front, a puppet show for the masses, whilst behind the scenes, though not totally out of sight, the real elite are putting the pieces together for global governance with their army of trained leaders. Of course, it's all for our benefit. For more information on this enormous subject go to: www.ukcolumn. org/series/one-world-governance.

A classic example of how this works is how the Rockefellers took total control of medical science thorough the Flexner report in 1910. This report, funded by the Carnegie family, came back to basically state allopathic medicine and germ theory were the only scientifically accepted way of thinking, and therefore acting in terms of disease. This report was then financed by the Rockefellers who took total control over medical schools and science. It is now not possible to qualify as a medical doctor if you do not agree with their thinking. This thinking then went on to create the WHO and now this one organisation and one family have a monopoly of truth with regards to health and disease. This truth has not only made them billions of dollars, but has now given them total control over humanity. If you challenge the truth then you are simply kicked out of the club.

If you wish to get involved in local community projects, be sure to look at who is controlling the agenda. Only a true grass roots, non-controlled community group deciding for themselves, and without imposing their ideas on others, will protect us from being infiltrated by these "useful idiots" from the global leadership programmes. With masses of propaganda and psychology being thrown at us from all angles, too much to consciously process, the only way to not fall under the spell is to remain aware of your own personal balance. *Know Thyself* and the rest does not matter.

A tale of two policemen

Here I am about to give you an example of how these training programmes have affected the minds and therefore the behaviour of public servants at ground level. These public servants may or may not have been through any "common purpose" course, but there is a high chance they would have been trained in their job by someone who has. For many years, psychological profiling has been used for picking candidates to work in public service, whether that is the police, NHS, education, and more. The idea of this is to get the "right" candidate for the job. The training that goes on in all public sector areas is all set up to give the workers the same mind-set, and there is no room for free thinking. Here are two conversations I had with two experienced policemen about ten years apart. The difference in attitude is striking.

Policeman one

About ten years ago I was chatting to a newly retired policeman I knew. He was a nice guy, a family man and well liked. I asked him a simple question, "Do you believe we are becoming a police state?" "No," was his simple answer. I explained my reasons for asking and he went on to tell me that when he was on duty, when he was in the force, he was trained to react to a situation using common sense. He would arrive at an incident, and if it could all be calmed down, then a solution could be found peacefully, then he was allowed to use his own discernment and make a decision based on common sense. He told me that at the end of his service he was taking young constables out on-the-beat, and when confronted by a situation, they just wanted to follow the rule book. They had given up their own ability to reason and use common sense, and just did what the rules told them. Knowing what I know, I find that a very telling piece of information.

Policeman two

A month or two into lockdown in the UK in 2020, I was chatting to a policeman who was off duty. Again, a nice guy, a family man and well liked. He already knew my opinion about what I felt was really going on. I mentioned to him the excess deaths that had occurred after lockdown began, and that were caused clearly by the lockdown policies. I then went on to quote him how the politicians were using a team of psychologists to create fear amongst the population so they would accept the rules. I told him he could easily find proof of this on the government website. This is what I quoted him: "The perceived level of personal threat needs to be increased among those who are complacent, using hard-hitting emotional messaging." From a document published by the UK Government called "Options for increasing adherence to social distancing measures" (22nd March 2020). I mentioned to him that many people were dying at home from heart attacks, strokes, and more, as they were too afraid to call an ambulance to go into hospital. His very clear reply followed: "That's their own fault then, isn't it?". When I queried him about the surveillance state, he also gave the Orwellian reply of: "If you are doing nothing wrong then you have nothing to worry about". This is what decades of trained leaders and psychology being used on the public has done. Even George Orwell would have been impressed. This explains the actions of the police worldwide being turned against the people they claim to serve. This explains military police attacking and beating unarmed peaceful protestors in Victoria State, Australia in the name of "keeping them safe".

A recommended book to read is *Waco – A Survivors Story* by David Thibodeau. It tells of a horrific incident that did not need to happen, but did, because of the mind-set of the people in charge, and the lack of any thinking at all by the order-following military police.

Salesmen of the lie

The UK Government Cabinet Office published a document entitled *MindSpace, Influencing behaviour through public policy*. The document, in simple terms, is how psychology can be used, and is being used, to sell government policies to the public.

Edward Bernays was the nephew of Sigmund Freud and was the first to use psychological techniques in public relations. His work and techniques have been used in advertising and by government policy makers worldwide. In simple terms they are sales techniques.

Taken from the MindSpace document.

"We outline nine robust influences on human behaviour and change. These principles are underpinned by considerable research from the fields of social psychology and behavioural economics. They are therefore presented as the most robust effects that policy-makers should understand and, if appropriate, use. The following sections briefly explain these effects, which we have arranged according to the acronym: *mindspace*."

Messenger: we are heavily influenced by who communicates information

Incentives: our responses to incentives are shaped by predictable mental shortcuts such as strongly avoiding losses

Norms: we are strongly influenced by what others do

Defaults: we "go with the flow" of pre-set options

Salience: our attention is drawn to what is novel and seems relevant to us

Priming: our acts are often influenced by sub-conscious cues

Affect: our emotional associations can powerfully shape our actions

Commitments: we seek to be consistent with our public promises, and reciprocate acts

Ego: we act in ways that make us feel better about ourselves

So governments are openly using psychology to socially engineer the public. By getting into our minds and installing beliefs and perceptions, they are taking away any possible freedom of thought, and with constant fear, they are disconnecting us from our intuitive knowing. They are selling us into slavery on a worldwide scale.

If we go back to the Garden of Eden and the seduction of Eve by the serpent, we can see Eve was not forced or coerced, and the knowledge of good and bad was not pushed down her throat. The serpent sold Eve a lie. It was a sales pitch any second-hand salesman would have been proud of. If we go back to the illustration of life as a video game, it could be said that Adam and Eve were living in full connection with creation.

They were being guided by the Creator and using their own minds to consciously experience this reality on earth. Using their conscious minds and their brains for what they were meant for, and leaving the guidance to the nature they were created and formed by. We could then easily state that Eve was being sold the lie that she knew better than creation itself. She was sold the lie that she could live outside of the boundaries of her creation and things would be better. She was just missing out on too much. This is kind of like the stage a teenager goes through when they think their parents do not understand them and they know better. You can see this as Eve chose her own thinking ability over the knowing and wisdom she was created out of. Artificial Intelligence over natural intelligence!

With this disconnection clearly seen in humanity now, it could be said we have become lost in the game, and instead of playing the game, we are being played by the game.

As it was Eve who was tempted, you could also see this as a loss of spiritual connection through our feminine side and the domination of our earthly masculine side. It would then mean that all the suffering mankind has gone through, and continues to go through, is not a punishment from God, but a consequence of living a life not in balance with how we were created, and going beyond the boundaries of what nature has given us. The teenage rebellious years of thinking – "I know better" – have caused enough damage and it may be time to grow up.

The controllers of the artificial system, represented by the serpent, are still selling us the lie and the slavery that goes with it. They are dependent upon humanity relying on their own thinking, with a mind they have programmed themselves. They could not control a humanity being guided by nature. They are selling us a lie, and in a reality of free will, they are entitled to do that. What they are selling is not important. The important question is, what are you buying?

HUMAN RIGHTS
VS NATURAL RIGHTS

Most people consider human rights and the UN Declaration of Human Rights as a great thing for mankind. With the whole world signed up to protecting these rights, what could go wrong? In theory, all governments around the globe should be working hard to protect the freedoms and the security of the people they claim to serve. The actual reality is the total opposite, to the point where now they even claim the right to tell you how to breathe, when you can leave your house, who you can meet, and what medical procedures you need to take to get back the freedoms they claim to have given you. At the same time, they have taken away those freedoms. Let's take a look at some of the rights we have under this declaration.

UN Declaration of Human Rights

Article 1

"All human beings are born free and equal in dignity and rights. They are endowed with reason and conscience and should act towards one another in a spirit of brotherhood."

On the surface this looks fine, but we need to look a little deeper. Defining words is what is left out. How do you define "born free", what do they mean by "rights", and who defines how we should "act"?

Article 4

"No one shall be held in slavery or servitude; slavery and the slave trade shall be prohibited in all their forms."

It seems the people who created this right, and signed up to it, have no understanding of debt slavery and how free-trade has created slavery all over the world

Article 5

"No one shall be subjected to torture or to cruel, inhuman or degrading treatment or punishment."

I don't think this one applies to Julian Assange.

Article 6

"Everyone has the right to recognition everywhere as a person before the law."

This right to be regarded as a "person", and therefore a member of the official society, has now become an obligation. You have no choice.

Article 19

"Everyone has the right to freedom of opinion and expression; this right includes freedom to hold opinions without interference and to seek, receive and impart information and ideas through any media and regardless of frontiers."

Here it is clear we are only free to think what we are told to think, with anything but official truths being censored. The mass control the mainstream media and government now have over information should be obvious.

The above examples of rights clearly show where rights we are told we have are simply being ignored and not being respected or protected. The next sets of rights show how an actual right can become an obligation and that the only people allowed to define these rights are the political leaders.

Article 26

"(1) Everyone has the right to education. Education shall be free, at least in the elementary and fundamental stages. Elementary education shall be compulsory. Technical and professional education shall be made generally available and higher education shall be equally accessible to all on the basis of merit.

(2) Education shall be directed to the full development of the human personality and to the strengthening of respect for human rights and fundamental freedoms. It shall promote understanding, tolerance and friendship among all nations, racial or religious groups, and shall further the activities of the United Nations for the maintenance of peace.

(3) Parents have a prior right to choose the kind of education that shall be given to their children."

So how do we define all of that?

Anything that is "compulsory" means you have no choice, meaning you are not free. Who decides what the "full development of the human personality" even means? As for parents having the "right to choose", it seems they are only able to choose from the options they are given.

Many countries in Europe do not allow home education, and countries where it is allowed, the restrictions and tightening are plentiful. In the UK, home-schooling was never defined, and people were free to do as they wished. The laws are about to change with a forced register of home-schooled children. A system of forced registration normally applies to sex offenders. So home-schoolers are now in the same risk category of sex offenders. Is there any evidence that home-schooled kids are at risk? On the contrary, there is simply no evidence. If there was, it would be all over the front page of the newspapers. In state schooling now, sex education is compulsory with "masturbation and sexual experimentation" and gender ideology fully on the curriculum for children after the age of five. This is where a right becomes an obligation, then becomes a total fascist attack. The Incas in Peru had no known written language, yet they were renowned for being expert engineers and farmers, and created an empire that conquered people with what it could offer. Yes, a threat of force was still there, but their empire grew because of their knowledge.

The idea of one curriculum for every country, every region, and even every child, is absurd unless you see it for what it really is. And that is a system for indoctrination of people to accept a system of control.

Article 29

"(1) Everyone has duties to the community in which alone the free and full development of his personality is possible.

(2) In the exercise of his rights and freedoms, everyone shall be subject only to such limitations as are determined by law solely for the purpose of securing due recognition and respect for the rights and freedoms of others and of meeting the just requirements of morality, public order and the general welfare in a democratic society.

(3) These rights and freedoms may in no case be exercised contrary to the purposes and principles of the United Nations."

Straight away we can see that now we are given "duties". So we have gone from a declaration of freedom to having "duties". Then we have the issue of immoral people preaching about "morality". They alone are able to define "public and general welfare". And as for the "purposes and principles of the United Nations" that is a clear statement that we are, in effect, to do as we are told.

The last human right I feel is important has not yet been put into law. It is the "right of health". These are the words now being spoken about by the WHO. Sounds great I know, but again who defines health? Who defines how we get to be healthy? As we know, they are totally controlled by the Rockefeller family and Mr Bill Gates, who between them, run the whole of big pharma and vaccine industry. This can only mean one thing, and that is why the book *Medical Fascism*, has the title it does. With the WHO at this very moment drawing up plans for the whole world to sign up to a "Pandemic Treaty", this will turn medical fascism into medical tyranny with one man, Bill Gates, able to lockdown the whole world if he and his germ-team just think there may be a "novel virus" threatening mankind.

I hope this short chapter shows you how human rights given to humans by other humans can only lead to enslavement. We have natural rights totally above the illusion of man-made rights. To embrace our natural rights, we have to see through the smoke screen of a fake system, and see the actual truth and reality of where we are from – nature itself.

GIVING AND RECEIVING

With every individual now having become free, and taking responsibility for their own lives, it may call up images of complete and utter chaos. All individuals, at any moment in time, wandering off in all directions, doesn't immediately conjure up a picture of *togetherness*. How can we be together if we have different needs, at different times, taking actions to fill in those needs? And won't all these needs directly invoke conflicts everywhere? Free individuals needing different things – it's not about wanting – and "having the right" to do whatever is required… to fulfil those needs will unavoidably bump into one another, and clash over whose need is the greatest, and over who got there first? It may make you wish for a prison environment where it is warm, safe and predictable. But life isn't predictable. At least not if you don't understand how it functions.

And if you do understand it, you know that every organism must possess an intrinsic freedom of choice and action. It works in nature, but what is the problem then for humans? What makes it different for humans to live together in comparison with animal troupes?

Animals only live in the here and now. They are directly connected to what is happening right now in their lives, and they do not project ideas and beliefs into the future, as they neither keep dragging the past into the present. They have learned lessons from their past experiences, but they are not holding grudges or blaming others. They have learned lessons which have led to a change in behaviour, but none of those lessons are being made personal. It is about what happened to them, not about who they consider to be responsible for what happened. Their behaviour changes and that is the end of it. How the learned lesson came about becomes irrelevant after the event. Only the lesson is important, not the circumstances in which one learns the lesson. Human lives are different in a fundamental aspect.

The human mind is differently constructed from all creation that precedes humanity. It has the capability of creating a separate reality from the one life is unfolding in.

A human being can imagine things, situations, and feelings. We are the only living organism that adjusts our individual life to what we believe others are thinking about us. We create an entire way of living together, based on opinions, our own and others. Opinions – what we believe – dominate both the structure and the functioning of human society, unlike any known animal society or community. It goes from believing a good schooling will lead to a good job, one that provides us with a "decent" financial platform, to the belief that money helps to create a good life, and with a good life we mean a life in which we are not troubled too much by disturbing experiences.

All are opinions and beliefs, none of which relate to a natural reality. All such opinions have been induced by humans for humans, by the organisers of human society, by the individuals that want to bring people together around the themes that are important to them, such as industrial success or social status.

It is what benefits certain people, who have a common interest, who form a certain layer within society, that steers the rest of the group, or humanity, in a specific, by the steering group, well laid-out direction.

In order to achieve this feat, this manipulation of the masses, the steering individuals need their opinions to become accepted by the rest of the population. This requires the introduction of experts, of people that other people believe do know more than they themselves know. Once you have experts, and you achieve that your opinion becomes the accepted truth amongst the population, you can bring people together where and when you want.

The people won't even notice the manipulation they have been subjected to because the "opinion" is being presented by highly recommended experts, whose opinion has been placed beyond reasonable doubt, in effect, beyond reason and beyond doubt. Opinions have been turned into truths right in front of everybody's eyes and people do not realise they have been tricked. It is a magic show in the purest form.

This results in a human society that is based on what, to all intents and purposes, can only be called an illusion. Certain beliefs, certain opinions, have been elevated to the status of truth, and form the basis on which the population is now being moulded into a society. The foundation for this society is laid by people who believe they know what is best and they have managed to convince almost the entire population of their opinion. So with the approval and the cooperation of the population, the accepted opinion becomes the truth that everybody knows. Or so it is being presented.

However, when we are looking at nature, the structure within which humanity has been created, none of those beliefs or opinions are actually present. In nature, no money is needed.

No organised schooling is to be seen anywhere. There does not exist exclusive ownership. What we do find in nature is hierarchy within certain communities. We also find working relationships within certain groups of animals and between various animal and plant species. In the wider picture, we notice that everything has a purpose and that there is harmony and symbiosis between all life forms.

There is indeed a struggle for survival, but this is secondary to sharing living space and food. Within nature we also recognise the duality at every level: all living organisms are at the same time predators and prey. Life is a perpetual dance of giving and receiving.

Humanity, on the contrary, is focused on "rights" that people believe they possess. If that is indeed the case, such rights have been granted to them by other people, not by nature. This can easily be seen in the fact that doctors have rights other people do not possess, such as the right to diagnose a disease, and the right to decide when someone's life has lost its value, and should therefore be terminated.

Each group that has been formed within society has been given special rights, as can be seen in the police force, the military, judges, teachers, politicians, actors, and so on. Your profession comes with privileges, with certain rights, but humanity has also created rights for the systems and institutions they have set up. Banks have rights that individuals do not possess. So have oil companies, governments, electricity companies, pharmaceutical companies, trade companies, food manufacturing companies, and so on.

Companies are formed by people and are given the same status as an individual with regards to human laws. Human laws are invented by people who tell others what they have to adhere to, what is acceptable to the organisers of society, and what isn't. Humans are handing "rights" to people and to institutions they have created, which gives these humans control over the other people and over institutions. Giving rights, limits the scope of the lives of the people who receive these rights, because, by stating what you are allowed to do, it directly also indicates what you are not. Giving rights to people actually puts their lives in a manufactured cage.

In nature, the only right any organism has, is the right to live. Intrinsically, every organism has been built to maintain life as long as it is possible. Every organism knows intuitively what it requires in order to give it the best possible chance to survive. It is called the intrinsic natural healing. However, for such a life to be present, it needs to be in harmony with its environment.

This means that the environment must not be disturbed by that life to such an extent that the surroundings it lives on, and in, are being pushed out of balance. So the organism can feed itself, but not deplete the food store. If it does, nature will be unable to continue reproducing its food and so the organism will bear the consequences of its actions. In real terms, this means that the organism has the responsibility to respect its environment while it tries to stay alive.

Staying alive to the detriment of your environment is only going to end up in your own destruction. So, yes, you have the right to live, but that life is not worth more than your surroundings. There has to be a balance, so both can survive in the long term. One single life is not worth living, when, by living, it destroys its environment, which will be the death of it anyway. The environment ultimately determines how far the right to an individual life stretches. Hence, "demanding" the right to live is ludicrous without taking the responsibility for that life.

Human society focuses on your rights, while nature focuses on your responsibilities. You need to live a responsible life, which means that you take your life in your own hands, and that you are responsible for what you do and how you do it. Natural tribes have always known this and lived by it. They will gather food, but they will ensure they leave some for nature too. Their lives are ruled by what they need, not by what they want, or have a right to. Life itself, in its entirety, is much bigger than a human life.

Life consists of a lot more than a human being. An individual organism will naturally strive to survive, which allows the species to survive. If you want to be part of life, of living, then you need to respect life as a whole and not enforce the rights you believe you have upon other lives. You need "to earn" your place within the structure of nature, within the complete picture of life.

For instance, there is no life at all without microscopic organisms, and no complexly constructed life without insects. They provide the basis on which all plant and animal life has been created and develops. So killing them off because they are a nuisance to you, eventually will lead to the destruction of your own life. It is recognising this relationship that entitles you to a place within the living community.

We need to understand that it is vital to live in harmony with living organisms and nature in general. Once we realise that the main question becomes "how we can sustain our life in relation to, and in harmony with our environment, with nature?", it is then that we can begin to see the real picture of our integration and our anchorage in nature.

The answer is very simple. We need to focus on giving. It isn't about what we can take from our environment. It is about what we can give to our environment, what we can contribute to nature, which we are an integral part of. So whether we are talking about a human life within the natural environment, or we are talking about a human life within the human environment, the principles of nature, the principles of life, remain the same.

In order to have any chance of living a harmonious life, and getting the most out of each individual life, that life, that human being, needs to give to its surroundings, including other humans, what it can. It needs to contribute to the lives by which it is surrounded. So giving then becomes the most important thing in life. And here too a balance needs to be maintained. Don't give away anything that is essential to your own life because otherwise you will undermine your own life and you may even make it impossible for your system to continue.

But here lies the biggest challenge for humanity at this point in its development. Human beings as a new creation have begun life, just individual human babies, demanding and grabbing everything they can get their hands on. Taking all they can in order to satisfy their hunger, and as long as the environment allows this, the baby and toddler have no idea that there are limits to what can be taken.

Humanity as whole is at this stage of its development. The growing child can only learn that certain things are no longer acceptable if and when their environment calls a halt to their grabbing, to their taking without any consideration for the effect it may have outside of them. We need to learn this. We need to be confronted with the shortcomings of our behaviour. We need to observe that gathering stuff in one place, in one life, depletes other places of that stuff. We shift things around whereby one life becomes easier to maintain, and the lives and natural resources, that life is built upon, become impossible to maintain.

As all of nature is connected, and influences each other, the collection and securing of living resources in one place will have its effect in other places. The habit of taking things away has its natural limits for our own lives. Nature has its limits. It also requires certain conditions in order to live, in order to sustain life, and placing ourselves outside or above nature is inevitably going to result in the destruction of our own life, as nature, the framework we have been created in, will react to preserve its own life, its own sustainability, its future.

So humanity needs to make a shift from taking to giving. We need to work our way up to becoming young adults instead of small children. We need to take responsibility for our lives, for our actions, and we need to learn to consider the real consequences of our actions.

Humanity is the total sum of human individuals. So a human being needs to learn to give rather than to take. But on the other hand, each life needs to take whatever it requires to carry on living. If an animal does not want to kill a plant or another animal, it won't have any food, and therefore it will die.

So there are needs on the inside of every life and there are needs on the outside of that life. In both worlds, life needs to be able to continue as one depends on the other. Nature also depends on which individual lives, and which species are surviving, in order for it to shape the environment of all living organisms. And this becomes the real challenge, as we are not used to taking the outside world into consideration.

We have been living in an illusion that we need and are able to fulfil our wants. What we wish for we should strive for. What we wish for is the driving power behind our lives. We put a lot of effort into achieving our goals in life. But as humanity as a whole is only at a child's development stage those goals are determined by what the child wants. When it wants an ice cream it will be happy when it gets the ice cream. Every other situation will create dissatisfaction and even anger directed towards the force that the child believes is obstructing the child from getting what it wants. Whether or not it actually needs an ice cream is completely irrelevant. This kind of life is no longer sustainable.

The first important switch we need to make is to turn away from what we want and to learn to replace it by what we truly need. A need is rooted in survival. A want is a desire that has its origins in our brain. And the brain is the place where human beings create an illusionary world, where they reason, and construct an image of life in the way they want it.

In order to satisfy these wants, in order to manifest this illusionary world, we need to remove everything we require from our environment, keeping only one picture in our mind and that is to match our reality with that of our dream. This way of living focuses on taking and taking until we have reached the point where our illusion looks to have become reality. Once we reach that point, the brain conjures up a new goal, a new aim, a new illusion for us to reach out to. And we start grabbing again in order to satisfy our new desire. Until we get stopped by our surroundings, which we are depleting constantly, we are not aware of any "wrong-doing". We are not aware of any imbalance we are pursuing.

It is time to wake up and to grow up. We do not need to wait for nature to revolt against our behaviour and to stop this. Instead of having to feel the pain of being refused the things we need in order to satisfy our childish fantasy, we could become aware of what we are actually being in the process of. Waking up to the fact that we are taking far more than we actually need in order to live "a good life" allows us to make the necessary changes to our behaviour without having to go through the pain of dealing with being denied what we are pursuing.

We need to learn how to give.

Nature provides everything every life requires. However, if one life takes from that rich treasure much more than it actually requires, it effectively denies other lives access to essentials they need.

We need to stop this. We need to start with recognizing that most of what humanity is living on nowadays is based on their imagination of their requirements. Mostly we have lost contact with the essentials of living requirements.

So the first step we have to work on is to stop "wanting" things in life. We need to learn to relax rather than to be afraid of missing out on something, or of having a shortfall of something. Because we have been trained to want more all the time, we fail to judge the real value of our requirements.

Life still continues happily without a telephone, a car or a television set, even without a job. You do not die when you lose your job! Stopping ourselves from desiring things that are not present in our current life is a first essential step in this process. If we don't make this decision and live by it, we will never truly get to the bottom of life, to the real essentials of life.

Recognise your desires for what they are and observe the difference between essential and non-essential. Do this on a daily basis. In winter time, being able to make a fire in order to keep warm may be an essential element of life, while this may not be the case in summer time. And what has this got to do with giving?

What we do not need we do not take. This means it becomes available to others. We allow others to take, to use, whatever we do not need at that time. So when I am not mowing my lawn I do not need the lawnmower, which means that my neighbour can use it if he needs to cut his grass. If I do not need to eat, then the bread that is there can be used by someone who is hungry and needs to eat.

Instead of reducing our fear of having too little by gathering more and more, we trust that life will provide us with what we truly need. This opens the gates towards not possessing anything beyond our true requirements and allowing others to take, right from under our noses, the things that we might need tomorrow.

This idea of what we might require tomorrow is a projection born out of fear, created in the brain. We imagine what tomorrow could look like and we want to cover our possible needs for those circumstances. However, those circumstances are not real today, and are not real tomorrow, unless they really are happening tomorrow. If that is the case we can deal with them tomorrow, but today it is not a reality. What we are doing here is filling in our needs for today and adding filling in needs we possibly might have tomorrow. If we keep doing this, we may require everything at some point in our life and so we are unable to give anything.

We really need to hold on to everything we have, everything we own, and we need to get hold of everything else in case we need it sometime in the future. This attitude pulls the resources into one place, depleting other places of these resources, creating poor to impossible living conditions for others. This is true in nature as it is in a human society.

To allow life in general to flourish, we need to learn to give things, to allow other living organisms access to the same resources that feed our own life. When life around us flourishes our own life becomes enriched too. Life itself creates more life as that is the purpose of life, to perpetuate itself.

When you allow animals to feed of the nature's provisions you feed of, more life will be created. When you allow insects to live in the same garden, in the same field, as you do, they will provide pollination to your plants which allows your fruits and vegetables to flourish. When you allow other animals into that same space, they will feed themselves on the animals that are already there, whereby they ensure that the space will not be overcrowded by a certain species.

Nature already has a balance and it doesn't need our thoughts on the matter in order to sustain life. It already knows how to do this. It is up to us to recognise this and to allow this into our lives.

When human beings are able to forget about the rights they believe they have, and they begin to observe how nature functions in balance and harmony, they themselves can merge into this balance if they adhere to the rules of the ruling power. Nature is the framework of all creation. We are part of that. We cannot escape that. If we manage to settle down and take our rightful place within that structure, we will discover that there is indeed a place for us. However, we need to bow down to the superpower nature is, and to the fact that it rules every form of life, including that of humans.

A human being, like every other life form, can provide for itself whatever it requires to sustain its own life. All the rest it leaves untouched. More so, like every other form of life, a human being can contribute something to life in general.

A human being can add value to another life by doing what it does best and allowing others to benefit from this. When a lion kills to feed itself and its offspring, it leaves a lot of food to a lot of other animals, even to plants. It takes what it requires and gives away all the rest.

Humans can learn to do too. We can give to others whatever we can do or know and, just like the lion, we can walk away from it without needing any compensation for our efforts. What we leave behind is a gift to others. It does not require any compensation because I already got my satisfaction from doing what I am good at, what I enjoy, what is useful to me. I am happy, without you, who now also benefits from my action, having to compensate me even more.

Every gift is a free gift. It is a donation for the good of others. The compensation I receive is twofold. I get immediate satisfaction out of doing what I am doing, and I know that whenever I need help, whenever I need the skills or knowledge of another person, I also will receive it. Whatever I truly need will be provided. If I don't receive what I think I require, it will encourage me to look at my situation in a different light. This will stimulate me to search for a different solution than the one I had in mind, and this process will enrich my life, broaden my scope, widen my arsenal of skills. No matter what happens, I always gain!

It is crucial that we human beings change our mind towards life. We need to change our belief about life. We do not need to fight life in order to survive. We need to embrace it and harmonise with it. We need to get rid of the idea that only the fittest will survive and enjoy the symbiosis within nature.

In nature nothing is without purpose or meaning, and that includes illness and death. We have chosen to fight these things, to believe these are things we do not need in our life. Maybe it is time for us to realise that pain and discomfort teaches us essential lessons about life and how to live. Instead of reacting from a child's perspective of life – "don't like it, don't want it" – we can choose to learn. Learning how to make giving the most important aspect of our lives is an essential step on our path to create more freedom in life.

Making that change within a human society that has been groomed to accept the concept that giving requires something in return is a huge exercise for any individual. Our society has evolved from a bartering system towards a financial system, but essentially both are the same. It always involves a system of debt. If you receive something you are indebted to that other person, and at some point, you need to "repay" him. An "I owe you" note of any kind is a symbol of this debt. A consequence of this system is that when you are unable to repay the giver, he is entitled to take what is rightfully his.

Who has given him that right? He himself, because he feels he has now lost something that he had before, whether it is goods he gave you, or provided you with a service. In our society we are even indebted to others for time they spend with us or for us. Also, any debt a person may have as a result of receiving something from another person, shows the value of the gift.

From the moment we, as a society, begin to value certain services and certain goods as having more value than others we begin to discriminate between the skills and knowledge individuals bring to this society. This creates a pecking order we do not find the equivalent of in nature. Nature does not value the contribution of a tree less than the contribution of an ant or a seagull.

Everything in nature plays its part and gets the same rewards for it: space to live in. It becomes part of a kind of harmony that is completely lacking from human society. So not allowing an individual access to all that he requires in his life, because humanity does not value his contribution as large enough, is a concept we need to ditch.

It seems to me that the concept of "giving" has been distorted completely. It used to mean to freely transfer possession, but I fail to connect that with the manner in which we currently in our society "give time" or "give advice" or "give one another a hand". The way we use the concept of giving in our society is certainly unknown in nature. In nature everything is free. The trees produce oxygen for free. All they want in return is that there is room for them to live in. If they are denied that space then nature will no longer have oxygen. It is simple. It is the knowledge that, when everything is freely given, everything will be available too, which provides that magical balance. A gift does not need a direct compensation because you are being "compensated" by the fact that everything you need is available to you. Maybe you begin to feel how the introduction of a concept, opposed to the natural concept, has turned our minds around and now makes it very difficult for us to embrace the reality, the natural concept, as the true one. It is difficult for us to open our hearts and minds to the belief that "all will be all right". We fear it might not be. We might want to try it, but we will keep a close eye on our surroundings, on our fellow human beings, and we will evaluate and judge their contribution in relation to our own efforts, as seen by ourselves. Others may see them differently and this is the cause of conflict and total misunderstandings.

The other side of this coin is to receive. We need to change our mind to allow ourselves to receive, free from the guilt of not being able to return the favour. We need to learn to open ourselves up to the opportunities that come our way and we need to allow ourselves to see the opportunities and use them. You are free to receive the gift another is offering you, but you are also free to refuse it. Someone may offer you, with the best of intentions, what they believe might be a help to you, but if you decide it isn't, then you simply refuse the gift. Here the same principles are adhered to. Only you can know what it is you require, but any person is free to offer you their assistance or not, as you are free to either accept their offer or not. Whatever decision is made by either has no long-term consequences and will not impact the relationship these people have. This requires a change in mind-set.

We need to push aside what we have learned, and how we have been made to live together, in order to clear the field for a totally new way of creating a human society, mirroring the natural way. We can use the natural laws we already have discovered as a guide, as lighthouses that can direct us away from our previous pitfalls. Here are some simple concepts that need to be included.

If I do not want to be indebted to anyone then nobody else is indebted me. There is no exchange of goods or services, only free gifts.

- If I want to be free to make my own decisions in life then everybody else has that right too. I take responsibility for my decisions and take note of the limitations my environment confronts me with.

- If I want to cover my basic needs in life then everybody else has that right to. If someone else's needs clash with mine then together we need to evaluate if those needs at that moment in time do have equal value in terms of direct survival, and either an agreement on how to proceed emerges or, on rare occasions, it may become a fight for survival.

The principal requirements of human life are the same throughout. A basic concept of not being judged by another human being means that you shouldn't do any judging either. Refrain from restrictive interference in any other life. Ensure that any direct interference you engage in is a free gift and nothing else. If you are not able to give somebody something they need, then don't do anything. Don't form an opinion about that other life. Let the other get on with whatever he/she needs to do.

When we keep our noses out of other people's business, how will we then be able to form a society? If it is still possible, what would such society look like?

BUILDING A NEW SOCIETY

Why would we want to do that? How many times in the history of mankind have people built a new society? What good has it done them? And anyway, what makes you think this new one will be better than all those that have already passed in the parade?

It would, indeed, make a lot of sense to carefully consider all those questions, and others too, before we embark on another road to nowhere. Maybe we shouldn't begin with what we want to create. Maybe it is better, in the first place, to take a good look at what we have. Can we learn from what has already been done in the past?

What is a society? How can we describe it?

A society is a group of individuals involved in persistent social interaction, or a large social group sharing the same spatial or social territory, typically subject to the same political authority and dominant cultural expectations. Societies construct patterns of behaviour by deeming certain actions or concepts as acceptable or unacceptable. In other words, certain behaviours are coerced by the ruling authority upon the population.

These patterns of behaviour within a given society are known as societal norms and they have been implemented by the government of the society, by the ruling power. There are various aspects to every society such as an economic structure, a social structure, a legislative structure, a political structure, and so on. All of these are said to benefit the individual as well as the group. It is claimed that it is a win-win situation as, by working together and being together, one can achieve so much more than one individual can ever aspire to by himself. It is said that one is safer in a larger group, that work becomes more efficient when it is done together, that in a group one can accomplish things and reach goals that are otherwise an impossibility.

As all of this may be true, the question then is, if indeed society provides a win-win situation for the group as well as for each individual member?

What we need to understand is the fact that the formation of this group is not individuals freely joining. This is a small group of people who form a society by implementing rules, by forcing and bribing individuals to join, and to be locked into the system. Furthermore, very often the group already occupies a territory, in which case everybody living in that space automatically becomes a member of that society. No free choice there.

Children that either are born out of parents that are members, or that are born within, a certain territory become automatically members of that society. No choice there either. So we can form societies by choosing to become part of a specific group of people (music society, literary society, theatre society, etc.) or societies can be formed by putting a fence around a group of people and telling them they belong to a specific society. In the first type you have a choice to join or not, to voluntarily subject to their rules or not. In the second type, nobody is asking you anything, but they make sure you're subject to their rules. And that is certainly the way societies on the world map have come into being.

So there are two very important characteristics about societies that we have to bear in mind. One is that if we want to build a new one, we can either give people the choice to join or not. The other one is that because it will be our society, we can determine the rules and every member will have to abide by them.

Building a new society would then effectively mean that it's the same, but with different rules. Indeed, that could be a different society but the question really is, "what have we changed?"

This question can clearly be answered by looking at human history. Many times over the rules of societies have been changed. Many times over the rulers implementing the rules have been changed. Each time it is said to be a win-win situation in so far that the group benefits as well as the individual from being joined together as a society. If that is truly the case then the question arises as to what the motivation might be to toss aside one society and to build another one. If the group was benefitting from the existing society, and all individuals were benefitting, why does it have to change then? Are we sure that the new society will increase the benefits on both sides of the spectrum?

Human history shows us that the flaw in the structure is the lie that lies at the bottom of the building, the lie that forms the foundations on which the building has been constructed. And that is that society is beneficial to both the individuals and the group.

If each member of the society has a free choice to be a part of the group, for whatever personal reasons that person may have, and if that member has a free choice to leave the society at any given moment in time, then one can argue that the individual only has to stay for as long as he or she feels that they benefit from the membership.

However, political societies do not offer that luxury to their members. Every individual is locked into a system, without their obvious consent and without a means to leave. Their membership of such a society has been enforced. On top of that, enforcement agencies ensure that possible escape routes are being blocked and attempts to leave are severally punished. Members of this kind of society do not have a choice to either subject to the rules or not. The rules are enforced upon them, whether they like them or they don't. It is this kind of society that does seem to have the recurring problem of one ruler, of one set of rules, being replaced by another, and each time society is supposed to benefit the individual member as well as the entire group. And each time there seems to be a very good reason to change to another ruler.

What is the driving force behind these events?

Why do people become so disenchanted with the existing system?

It is all to do with "enforcement". Implementing onto others what to you may seem like a good idea is never going to benefit everybody, simply because we are all different and we do have different needs in life. So whomever is doing the implementing, the enforcing, is surely benefitting themselves. If they are not, then they have no reason to desire a specific system of being and working together. So they set something up, implement the rules in order to hold it together, and they benefit. Does everybody within the group benefit? Well, nobody really had a choice in the matter. They were all forced to be within the group and to adhere to the rules. If they were given a free choice, they could have decided for themselves to either become a member or not.

And why would you choose to become a member of a group if there is no benefit to you at all? Why would you subject to someone else's rules of living if you do not gain any benefits at all? Human history does not allow us to collate such data as no ruling power has ever allowed people to freely leave the society they were coerced to be a part of.

And here is the simple explanation for this. The needs of every individual within a society differ from one another, and they are different from the needs of the group.

Take the example of a company. Indeed, we can see that if the company is doing well, making big financial profits, then all the workers can be paid a decent wage and they are economically doing well too. That is a real incentive for the workers to put all their effort into the job. But then what happens?

Now each of the workers wants to buy a new house, a bigger car, and take a second holiday during the year.

On the other hand, the company would like to upgrade their equipment, move into a nicer building, and set up a second plant.

The profits of the company are owned by the company, not by the workers, so the company has a free hand to decide what to do with it. They can either majorly benefit themselves from the profits or they can give it to the workers. It is entirely their decision, not the workers' decision.

The workers are part of this society, but they do not have a say in what benefits they receive and what needs the company is claiming are in fact unfair. It is, whether you like it or you don't, the other way around. The company decides, unchallenged, what they need and what the workers are being given. Don't forget who is the boss in this society!

What makes a society? Its members.

Who is in charge of a society? The founders of the society, not its members! The people who gathered members to form a society, irrespective whether these people had a choice to become a member or not, are in charge.

Hence, every society you form in this way will have inherent conflicts within them, as individuals all have different needs, and they can't all be met by the rules set by the authority that has organised the society. No matter what they promise. No matter how hard they try.

In order for a society to operate without conflicts, without infighting, truly be peaceful, every individual will have to be able to meet the needs they have at any given moment in time. An added difficulty to achieve this is that the needs change with changing circumstances. A twenty year old will have different basic need from a seventy-year-old person. And as we are all getting older our needs in life change. On top of that, everything around us, our environment, changes all the time too. So even if an authority today – let's for a moment follow this illusion – achieves to deliver, via their rules and regulations, a harmonious balance within the population, everything will be different again tomorrow and their rules will no longer have the same outcome. A society regulated by an authority is doomed to fail, viewed from the individual requirements.

The only other way to form a living community is to begin building it from the individual upwards. We have grown up, we have been trained, to accept an outside authority as a necessity in the formation of a living community. We believe that if there does not exist an authority that writes rules for everybody to adhere to, and also implements those rules, enforces them upon the individuals, that there is no standard for people to know what is right and what is wrong.

Nevertheless, nature has also provided us with an inherent sense of what is just and what is unjust. That is why we have a judiciary system that is supposed to deliver justice to its population. Anybody who feels that they have been treated unjustly can make a complaint. So every individual has a sense of justice within them. The only thing we find troublesome is that these individuals do not agree on what that justice actually entails.

To the predator it seems just to take the life of a young animal as there is nothing wrong in needing to feed its own offspring. On the other hand, to the mother that loses the youngster, it seems entirely unjust that she cannot raise her offspring. It doesn't get us anywhere trying to sit in judgement over the way this works. We didn't create it this way and we don't have any say in its operational aspects. We would do well to observe and to try and learn how it works rather than to judge it.

Every aspect of nature has its requirements. Every aspect of nature has its justification. It turns out that the requirements of no single aspect of nature are met all the time. It is a constantly shifting balance. The plants don't even get what they need all the time, when they need it. It doesn't always rain when they need it to. So this constantly shifting balance results in a system whereby you sometimes get what you need and sometimes you don't. That is one important observation. The other one is that it isn't up to the living organism to decide when it gets what it needs.

It is the environment that is what it is, that provides what is available and when it is available. Bringing this back to human life, this means that the environment creates opportunities and takes them away, irrespective of what the individual thinks about it.

So what does all of this mean? The environment has its own agenda, follows its own path. We, as individuals, are carried on this path and we, just like all other living organisms, have our own individual requirements for our survival. Attempting to manipulate the environment to deliver what we require when we require it is futile. One can achieve little adjustments but these are very limited, no matter how "developed" humans become. We can water our garden in times of a drought to make our crops grow, but we cannot create the water we need to sustain this behaviour. Ultimately nature decides what our living conditions are and we will be forced to accept those.

Nature, our living environment, is a creative process we do not control or even can influence in a balanced and sustainable way. An individual life within that environment has its own needs in order to continue living, needs that are sometimes met by the environment and sometimes not. This is the reality of life. This is how nature functions. Whether we like it or we don't, this is how it is for all of us, humans and other creatures alike. Humans believe they are "entitled" to the life they want, thereby completely ignoring the reality of life itself.

When we transfer this insight, this knowledge, to humanity and human communities, we can see the same conflicting requirements between the single individual and the human group this individual is part of.

The group provides opportunities and the individual has personal needs. This is very well illustrated in nomadic human societies. The group needs to be in different places at different times of the year in order to survive. So they are on the move at certain times of the year.

When an individual is old or sick, unable to make the journey, they together, the group and the individual, may decide that it is in the best interest for such an individual to be left behind while the rest is moving on. This surely means that that individual will not survive for very long, but if the group either stays or puts the heavy burden on them to drag this individual along with them, none of them may survive. This is the balance in nature. This is the balance in life. This takes into account that life ends somewhere and that a futile attempt to save one puts the lives of the entire community in jeopardy.

Life is about keeping the balance between the needs of an individual and the needs of the group. The group needs to do what is best to them, and the individual needs to do what is best to the individual. How can this work when those needs are not the same, or even worse are opposite to each other?

In the example given it is clear that there is an understanding, both within the individual and the group, of the reality of their situation. It is this understanding that makes it possible for them to decide the best course of action without creating a conflict of interest. The individual concerned knows he is not going to survive. However, he also realises that in order for him to live a little longer, the safety and survival of the entire community will be put in serious danger.

A mutual understanding of the reality of the situation is needed in order to avoid conflict. This is how nature operates.

So why can't humans operate like that? Or can we?

The only thing that is required for us to do this is a true understanding of nature, of life itself. An understanding, not an emotion. If we understand the importance of what we, as an individual, feel we require, and of what the group requires at the same time, then it should be much clearer as to what is the right thing to do.

The basic requirements of an entire group outweighs the individual needs in certain circumstances. This doesn't allow the group to enforce its requirements upon an individual, because we are only referring to the basic needs of a group in order to survive.

A group should refrain from artificially creating more needs than nature implies, just as an individual should refrain from creating wants above needs. At the same time, if the survival requirements of an individual are such that the group can provide those specific circumstances without bringing the entire survival of the group in danger then it should do so, because a society only exists because of its members. In short, the members have to look out for the survival of the society and the society has to look out for the survival of each member. It can only work as a balancing act, without anybody having the authority to enforce one idea upon others.

Let's then have a look at how those two, frequently opposing requirements, can meet up to form a balanced living condition. Individuals have fundamental differences inasmuch that some may prefer to live in large communities and others in small ones.

Some may have a need to live by the sea and others way up the mountain. Some need a lot of personal space and others require little personal space. Some want more sunshine and others want less.

We can keep going to create more and more differences within the human race. If every single individual needs to try and meet their inner requirements, the basic elements on which to build that individual life, then it makes sense that they choose other individuals who have similar needs. This will avoid fundamental conflicts within the group, within their society. They all agree on a set of basic "rules", even without having to write them down or having to implement them. Everybody within such a group will automatically assume that everybody agrees on these terms and conditions. This simplifies living together as they can allow others to do as they would do themselves and they understand what other individuals are trying to do for themselves.

So, for starters, individuals need to be allowed to choose a community of people with very similar basic living needs. Everyone should have the freedom to make this choice for themselves. When over time such an individual changes, wants a different kind of life, he has the freedom to leave the community in search of another one that corresponds better to what he himself wants in his life at that moment in time.

Freedom to choose your community.

Freedom of movement.

The key point when we want to create a society, a way of living together, that has no human authority dictating the rules, is understanding. We need to understand the reality of life, the reality of creation, the reality of nature. Once we do that, we can easily see that what we require for ourselves is also *a basic right* to others. If I need the freedom to make my own decisions, then I need to understand that others also require that same freedom. From this point onwards I realise that I have no right to tell someone else what to do, when to do it, or how to do it. And nobody else has a right to tell me either.

When a number of people, that feel they basically want life to be organised in a very similar way, join together in order "to make work light", then they already have removed potential disagreements from their community.

The next level is, of course, the fact that within such a freely chosen group all individuals are still very different. The next thing to understand is that the same natural law applies at all levels. So individual differences need to be allowed and no individual should have any power or any say over any idea or action of another individual.

Each individual, however, will take responsibility for their own feelings, thoughts, words, and actions. All of these will have consequences within their environment, in other words within their community. As a result of the reactions of the community to the individual, that individual needs to evaluate his own actions, words and feelings within that community.

The individual has the choice to either readjust or to stick with it. If, however, the community keeps opposing, keeps blocking, the individual then a discrepancy arises between the direction the group is moving into and the direction the individual is moving into.

As it is inappropriate and contradictory to nature to enforce an individual's will upon a community, such an individual will have to make a personal choice. Either, if he/she wants to continue living within that community it is time to drop what he/she is pursuing, or, if that individual wants to carry on pursuing what he/she believes in, then it is time to leave this community in search of another one that does allow room for those feelings, thoughts and actions.

This is not about "being right". It doesn't matter. Even if the individual in the long run will be proven to be right, when the community is not ready to accept that, to see it, then that person lives in conflict. Living in conflict creates disease, which means that both the individual and the community will begin to function badly, will start to deteriorate, will become ill.

A healthy, balanced, community is one that is made up of individuals that are living together harmoniously. This means that they all get on. It means that they all share basic beliefs.

Whether these beliefs are absolute truths, are natural laws, or not, is irrelevant. When they are not in line with the natural order of things the community will, at some stage, be confronted with this reality and it will have, at that time, the opportunity to grow and to evolve.

It is not the task of any individual to force another individual along a development path he or she isn't ready for. Every individual has a right to express himself, to be true to his or her own nature, have their own beliefs and to follow a path of their own choosing. Dragging others with him, against their will, or coercing others, or bribing others to support that individual's feelings, thoughts and actions will only lead to serious conflicts.

The focus of each individual must lie on minimalizing conflict. And within this concept it is vital to understand that the only real impact any individual can have is to evaluate his/her own contribution to the conflict. Take a good look at your own behaviour and never invest any energy in finding blame in another. For an individual, the way out of a conflict is always to make a choice between two different attitudes. One can either stay within the environment the current conflict occurs in, in which case one must refrain from expressing oneself in that particular way in order for the conflict to disappear, or one can leave the environment and change to another one where one's expression does not create the same conflict.

What does all of this look like in terms of a society?

We have a group of individuals who have freely chosen to live together, based on a common belief and a common goal. These are small local groups as every group that forms itself naturally, organically, from the roots upwards, will be different in some respects.

There is no need for equality and sameness. In fact, that would be detrimental to a balanced life and to the health of individuals as well as the groups. These different groups respect their differences and the same understanding applies here. If one group has the right to do their own thing, to live life according to their own beliefs, so has another group.

No one group should enforce any ruling upon another. The groups have relationships with one another if and how they both are choosing this to be, but each group can maintain its own identity. No one individual is the boss within a specific group and no one group is the boss over another group. There is no authority. An individual relates to the rest of the group as that is the environment the individual lives in, and one group relates to the other groups within its neighbourhood as that is the environment that group lives in. It is the interactions between them that keeps the balance in life, in nature.

Just as an individual needs to look at his own impact on the community, each group needs to look at how they impact the groups around them. Situations that cause conflicts will have to be resolved from the inside. A group may not have the option to move away from the conflict, which means that they do need to seriously take into account how they impact communities around them. If need be, a group in conflict with another will need to alter how they express themselves in their outside world. Both groups within a conflict need to do this.

Such a society is built on two basic principles, nothing more.

1. Individual responsibility in all aspects of life
2. Respect for everything in life

Everything in life will be in your own hands and you will have to take care of it, carry the responsibility for it. If you do, you will be free of any authority apart from your own. Then you grant every other individual the same rights as you have claimed for yourself and you respect that right as you want others to respect your right.

There will be no outside judgement, not of someone by you, and not done by someone to you. The only judgement that exists, the only way to evaluate what you have done, is to observe the effects of how you express yourself within the environment you are in. According to the goal you wanted to achieve and the effect it actually has, you take responsibility for it, and if need be, you alter how you express yourself to the community.

This kind of society is for the individual, for all individuals, and it is by the individual, by all individuals, as that is exactly where the responsibility for the society lies.

You want freedom?

You need to take full responsibility in life.

You need to respect the freedom of others.

TRANSHUMANISM

What the hell is that?

Has any reasonable thinking human being heard of such a word? We have heard about humanism, which is described as: a system of education and mode of inquiry that originated in northern Italy during the 13th and 14th centuries and later spread through continental Europe and England. The term is alternatively applied to a variety of Western beliefs, methods, and philosophies that place central emphasis on the human realm.

In chemistry the adjective "trans" is used to describe an isomer in which the atoms are arranged on opposite sides of the molecule. In general, the adjective is used to indicate *being on the opposite side*, as seen in the word transatlantic. Ah, now I get it! Transhumanism is *being on the opposite side to humans*.

Where the hell is that?

Where can I go to find out? Where better than a website that actually tells you, as it is called www.whatistranshumanism. org? This must be "the bible" of transhumanism. Indeed, it tells me what is meant by it.

> Transhumanism is a way of thinking about the future that is based on the premise that the human species in its current form does not represent the end of our development but rather a comparatively early phase.

What a clever premise! I wonder who taught them that humanity, in its current form, is not at the height of its potential? Of course, we are only at the infant stage of development! Every scientist knows that! There is so much more to come. Nature has a lot more for us in store, you can rest assured. So that's that then. Transhumanism is "the belief" that humanity still has a great deal of development in front of it.

Yes but! And here come the clever clogs. They seem to think they have to do something about it themselves.

> Transhumanism is a class of philosophies of life that seek the continuation and acceleration of the evolution of intelligent life beyond its currently human form and human limitations by means of science and technology, guided by life-promoting principles and values.

It's a philosophy! The evolution of intelligent life is not a natural thing, which will show itself in good time. No, apparently it is not going to happen unless the intelligence of humans is actually using science and technology to promote those values and principles. Oops, they already seem to have forgotten what they said in the first paragraph, which is that human species in its current form is at an early phase of its development. Surely this also means that our current intelligence is at a pretty basic, child-like, stage. And now this philosophy promotes the idea that this child of a human being is going to guide us towards a higher intelligence. Well, I'll be damned!!

I'm intrigued! I want to take myself step by step through their argumentation. This will be interesting. Here we go.

> Transhumanism can be viewed as an extension of humanism, from which it is partially derived.

Sorry, it isn't an extension. Being the opposite is not an extension. Being the opposite is not "extending" where I am or what I am. It places me in a totally different position, namely the opposite position. I am "at the other side", which is not an extension.

> Humanists believe that humans matter, that individuals matter. We might not be perfect, but we can make things better by promoting rational thinking, freedom, tolerance, democracy, and concern for our fellow human beings.

If by "we" you mean people that guide other people and set up ways for them to live by, I would refer you back to the content of this book. It doesn't read so well. Where is the "rational" in our thinking if we are no longer allowed to think and are only meant to accept the line of thinking that is being promoted by the authority that governs our lives?

Where is the freedom in forcing entire populations into believing and acting in one particular way, thereby crushing all opposition to this specific way? Where is the tolerance in not allowing people to make decisions about their own lives and live the way they want to without causing any harm to anybody else? Why is democracy mentioned here? Because it is the most subversive form of a dictatorship (majority decides and everybody is forced to listen)? How much are you concerned about your fellow human beings if you never listen to them, never allow them to think and to act as they need to, never allow them room so they can provide for themselves all the things that were promised to them but never delivered?

Transhumanists agree with this but also emphasize what we have the potential to become.

Great. Not "we", but every individual has a potential to become. To become what exactly? Why is this omitted here? Because the potential of every human being can be reached by that human being *if and when he/she will be given the opportunity*. It is an inherent potential that is very difficult to deploy when the individual is blocked, obstructed and scared off from developing in the direction that the individual needs to.

Just as we use rational means to improve the human condition and the external world, we can also use such means to improve ourselves, the human organism.

Before talking about the improvements to the human condition rational means have brought us, it might serve us to take a good look at the state our rational world is in today. All peace and quiet, is it? All prosperous, is it? All neat and clean, is it? In fact, it is so good that our self-proclaimed leaders are just having social intercourse because of their lack of work, lack of pressing problems that require their interventions and their intelligence.

It is this same intelligence, which has created our disastrous society, they are proposing, no imposing, to use for the improvement of the human organism. I had no idea that there was a shortcoming in the human organism. I am, however, well aware of many shortcomings in the way humanity behaves, that same humanity that is going to tell me how to improve my "organism", my living entity, created by nature, not by humans.

In doing so, we are not limited to traditional humanistic methods, such as education and cultural development. We can also use technological means that will eventually enable us to move beyond what some would think of as "human".

Technology is going to move us beyond being human. Oh, oh, what will I become then, if I am no longer human? A robot? So they seem to "know" they can use technology to shift us out of being human. I get it that technology can create a virtual world, but I am also aware of the fact that there is no life in that virtual world. Not so long ago, the same people, who are now advocating to bring you into an imaginary world, were locking people up in mental asylums for this same reason, for living in a virtual world, in their own fantasy world.

What is all this? Not one sentence on the opening page contains any truth, any reality, as far as real life is concerned. We are nature. Nature created us, according to the rules by which everything else in the universe has been created. The human being is the latest development in a series that started roughly 13.8 billion years ago. And now a creature comes along that says to have the technology *"to advance"* life in order to fulfil all its potential. Where does that potential come from? From the machines?

There is a difference between inventing a machine that can lift more weight than a human can and a machine that tells a human how to live their life or how to create a new life. The world of machines is technology. Life is nature. One is artificial and the other is natural. It is incredible to hear that humans believe they can create perfectly normal functioning human beings without the aid of nature, when, to date, they have not succeeded in creating sea water that sustains the variety of life it does in its natural form.

The advanced technology humans possess is incapable of sustaining marine life over an extended period of time but they tell us they can create, out of nothing, a new human being. If you want to believe that, you believe in the power of artificial life. I can clearly remember when they told us that once they had set foot on the moon, they would begin to build a colony over there, creating an artificial atmosphere for humans to live in.

What happened to those plans? I even saw proposed drawings and descriptions of how life was going to be maintained and developed. The truth is that the human presence in space has taught us that we can only be there for a little while as our physical systems quickly start to deteriorate. We need to bring those people back within a certain period of time so their systems can recover. If we don't, they will die, either when they do return (too late) or when they stay out there. Humans cannot recreate nature, even though some humans – part of that new nature development stage, which is in its infancy – - believe they can. What we believe and what is real in life are clearly two different things.

Artificial Intelligence may be intelligent in terms of academics. The thinking capacity of such an intelligence, created by humans, may be beyond the thinking capacity of a human at this stage of its development. So, its capacity "to remember" data and its capacity "to link" data may far outreach human capacity at this moment in time. However, here is the point they are missing. Life is not about logic or academic intelligence.

Life is about intuition. It's about sensing, not in the way a sensor, including our own senses, works, but in the way extrasensory perception works.

Life, including human life, runs on automatic unconscious reaction patterns, which are partly inherent in our system and are derived from the experiences of our direct ancestors, and partly based on what our system has learned when we came into this world, and it had to find a way to survive.

Based on all that information, rooted within the history of our ancestors and within the situation of life as and when we entered it, humans quickly build reaction patterns that they use unconsciously, instantaneously, and most of all, perfectly, to suit the kind of system they actual have, with the capacities and the weaknesses as they truly are. These artificially intelligent people do not even recognise the fact that each individual human being is unique. They believe we are all the same and so they believe they can make a human model that will have all the good characteristics and none of the bad ones. Once again, can you please define good and bad here, please? Because nature does not have that.

It's not because a machine can move that it is alive. It also is not because a machine can make logical deductions that it is an artificial human being. *"I think, therefore I am"* is indeed a correct statement for a human being. However, it does not define *who* I am.

Who you are is a natural organism, sprung out of a natural soup of circumstances that creates a unique specimen of the human being that thinks. So the machine that thinks, therefore also *is*. Correct. But it is, and will always remain a machine, something totally different from a human being, simply because it comes out of a completely different set of circumstances than the human being does.

Nature is, in itself, an intelligent web of energetic interactions, following simple rules and laws over and over again. Because this web has already been worked on, has been woven, for 13.8 billion years it would be fair, I assume, to admit that it may be a little more complex than the newest invention of this intelligence claims to be able to control, recreate and turn independent from its original source, from life itself, from nature itself.

Either you believe that artificial intelligence is going to save the planet, is going to give eternal life to the human being, or you believe that life is a creation of nature, belongs to nature and is controlled by nature. The two, I am afraid, cannot go together. You cannot *transhumanise* society and at the same time live life in a natural way. One excludes the other. Artificial life is *opposing* nature, not "extending" it, and will therefore attempt to destroy it. The reason is very simple: nature cannot be controlled and "somebody" does want life to be completely controllable. Trying to step out of the natural laws and the natural system you were born into is, in the long run, not a sustainable proposition. We can fantasize but we cannot leave our natural world behind for any length of time and sustain life in its normal fashion.

A life built completely on logic is a prison that has cells you do not fit into. It has a prison regime that is impossible for you to adhere to. Why? Think about what is *considered* to be logical. Logic is defined as:

- A particular way of thinking, especially one that is reasonable and based on good judgement,

- a formal scientific method of examining or thinking about ideas

Logic is one particular way of thinking (one narrative!), and it is based on "good judgement". Judged by whom? By whomever determines logic. So what may seem logical to you, but not to an authority means it is time for you to shut up. Logic is a "formal" scientific method. Who decides which form that is? You? I don't think so! Hence, logic is controlled by an authority, whom decides *for you* how you must think or "formally" conduct science. It is this logic that leads to artificial intelligence, as it does not allow nature's logic as "a particular way" of being. This logic is controlled by a human authority and is accepted by the population as a whole, whereby they turn their backs on all other natural possibilities. So life, based on an imposed logic, gives a lot less living space to a living organism than nature does. It also does not allow any room for self-experiences, the natural way to learn things.

Logic forms the basis of artificial intelligence and the entire structure is built and controlled by a human authority. If they tell you what is logical in your life, and you no longer can decide that for yourself, you have become imprisoned in artificial intelligence. The paradigm is "*it is too dangerous to think for yourself*, so let a machine do it for you". Less mistakes are being made that way. Again, please define "a mistake"? Who is setting the standard? Who is being the judge? The other benefit to this system is that if you do not like the outcome the machine has provided you with, there is nowhere for you to go and complain and there does not exist a way to rectify it. The machine is always right, simply because it has more thinking capacity than you and I. It simply "knows" more!

None of this is about what is right or wrong. Is artificial intelligence wrong? From the authority point of view that creates it, because it needs it in order to continue and to extend control over the masses, it is an absolute must in the development of human beings. However, when you want space to learn about life, about your own life, room to make your own mistakes in order to learn from them, then artificial intelligence is not at all needed. In fact, it would seriously get in the way. This means that these two ways of progressing into the human future do not go together. They are mutually exclusive.

You better wake up to the fact that you will need to make a choice about which way you would like your life to go. If you are not convinced yet that you do need to make a choice, then I suggest you keep your eyes wide open and bear these words in mind.

Either you fully commit to a life within nature or you allow yourself to be taken out of nature, to become transhumanised. Either you choose to be a human or you will be pushed outside of the human life. It isn't *"beyond"* being human – words they like to use. "Trans" clearly means *"on the opposite side"*. Using the term "beyond" makes it sound as if you will be able to rise above being human, which is not where you will be heading at all. To crush humans, to dehumanise humans, to exterminate natural life because it is *beyond* human control is what is going to be needed if you want to end up "on the other side" of being human.

Humans need to learn to live *within* their environment, the surroundings that shaped them, formed them, and energises them.

If you choose not to want to do that then you truly put yourself outside of human life. You truly are taking your first steps towards becoming a transhuman. Have a good journey. I know I won't be seeing you again.

THERE IS NO-THING WE CAN DO

Since the expansion of the internet and the availability of mass information to a large number of the population, many people have figured out how the system of slavery works. This has led to people looking for an answer, a solution to free us. Since the penny dropped for me in 2009, I too have been searching for what can be done.

I remember coming across Common Law in 2010 and thought that may be a way out. After about one day of research I decided it was far too much work. If I had to learn all that to be free then I'd rather make the most of my slavery. The truth is there is not one problem that cannot be solved or that we don't already have the solution to, whether it is money, economy, environment, energy, health, and more. The problem is not lack of solutions but a lack of awareness, backed by the right mind-set within the population.

The first thing needed is to become aware of our slavery.
We need to make the decision of wanting to be free.
We need to understand the methods used to enslave us.
We need to understand our own role in our slavery.
We need to unpick our slavery bit by bit.

We need to accept that, only by taking a moral stance and by acting in accordance with our conscience, which we need to connect to first, will freedom be won.

We need to use the Nature that is within us as our guide.

- Overcome ignorance with awareness.
- Overcome immorality by becoming moral by connecting to the heart and your conscience.
- Overcome fear by taking action, take deep breaths and do something, no matter how small.
- Overcome apathy in the same you overcome fear, and if you decide not to do anything, *do not complain.*

Go with the natural flow of life, and stop trying to control what does not want, and cannot be, controlled. *Trust in Creation.*

The events happening in the world presently can be seen as an attempt by the system to bring about an acute cleansing challenge to bring us back into balance. It is your responsibility as an individual to embrace this challenge and evolve, and although you may help other people through this process, it is important to know that they are not your responsibility and they should be allowed to go their own path. So in this context what is known as Karma could just well be a consequence of not doing what is right in accordance with natural law, whether individually or collectively, and not a punishment from God.

You could see this consequence like a homeopathic message trying to awaken our system to a life out of balance. If I was a homeopath looking down on humanity, and seeing they had given all of their individual and collective sovereignty away to a group of elites, my homeopathic remedy would be fascism.

Maybe it is the hit on the head we need to awaken our true spiritual self. We need to look at this message and not shoot the messenger.

As stated by Mark Passio in his talks on Natural Law, the amount of freedom in a society is relative to the amount of morality within the people in that society. This is why there is "no-thing" we can do. We can only live life and respond to life in a moral way and by taking a moral stance. Doing what we believe to be right, regardless of whether it is deemed correct, legal or lawful. The more people take this stance, the less the system will have control over us. The system had enormous problems with one man named Ghandi. It could not cope with millions.

As Trevor Gunn pointed out, there are four possible outcomes when confronting illness. What we are seeing now can be seen as a development stage for humanity where our awareness of life and who we are wants to expand. In order to achieve that a massive clear-out of beliefs and perceptions is needed. How this ends is anybody's guess, but if we accept that free-will exists then whatever the outcome we choose will be just.

- Humanity resolves the illness and as a result their health is improved and they are stronger than they were before. They are less susceptible to those problems after the illness and more able to deal with them.

- Humanity resolves the illness but there has been no learning, as such, they are not stronger than they were before. They effectively carry on as they were before the illness, just as susceptible to succumbing to the illness as they were before.

- Humanities illness is not resolved and as a result the health of the individual is worse than before and they descend into a lower level of chronic illness, more susceptible than before.

- Humanities illness is not resolved and the patient is unable to react sufficiently to overcome the problem and dies.

EPILOGUE

For an individual to "awaken" it is necessary for him to understand that he is enslaved, both by nature and by the human construction he is part of. We can't escape the fact that we are part of the nature structure. In other words, it is impossible for a human being to live outside of it. So, the only option an individual has is to live in harmony with its environment, "his prison warden". Trying to minimalize conflict at all times is the task within life. Finding peace and harmony within the walls of that prison is what we are here for.

When you put another prison, another set of restrictions, within the permanent prison of our lives, you simply make it very difficult to realise that specific goal. If you restrict what that individual is allowed to do, you seriously limit the options he has to achieve his personal balance in life. This is our prison created by other humans. This is the prison that makes life impossible for the individual. Ideally, the individual needs to break out of the human imprisonment in order to live peacefully inside the natural prison.

The human prison comes in the form of a society with all its rules, regulations and punishment procedures. So it is obvious that, in order to live a balanced life, the individual needs to remove himself from the society he lives in. Any society. Why? Because all societies that we know are power houses. The purpose of each society is to enslave its citizens. Realising this means that the individual has awaked, has become conscious.

When conscious individuals decide to live together, to form a living community, to be a society, one has a conscious society of human beings. This is what we call *a conscious humanity*, a society of conscious human beings. For this to be achieved, individuals need to denounce any claim to power over other human beings. They need to know that it is morally unacceptable that a human being is being denied the opportunity to express life in the way he or she needs to. They need to truly embrace universal freedom. They need to know that the only prison rules they are required to adhere to are commonly known as the natural law.

A conscious humanity will allow groups of people, who voluntarily join together, to live the way the group sees fit.

A living group, a community, within a conscious humanity will allow every individual to live the way that individual sees fit.

A conscious humanity will allow individuals to search for the group that, according to their own judgement, suits their living needs the best.

A conscious individual will endeavour to live in harmony with his natural and human environment, making the changes that the individual deems necessary to achieve this. A conscious individual chooses his human environment to suits his or her needs.

A conscious humanity will endeavour to live in harmony with its natural environment, giving and taking only what it deems necessary, and taking full responsibility for all the effects that their actions have caused within that environment.

If you want to be part of a conscious humanity, you need to become a conscious human being who then joins other conscious human beings to build a conscious humanity.

Lightning Source UK Ltd.
Milton Keynes UK
UKHW021431150123
415309UK00011B/126